Tyler was out of control—I had to stop him from taking my daughter...

Before I could even react, he snatched Madelyne out of my arms and put her in the back of his car. She started to hyperventilate.

"What are you doing?" I screamed.

Tyler ignored me as he tried to strap her in the car seat.

"Tyler! She's terrified! You can't do this! Let's take her to a park or something. She has to calm down before she can go with you!" Was he crazy? How could he do this to his own child?

I squeezed in between him and the doorframe of the car door. "Tyler! Stop!"

"Don't touch my fucking car!" Tyler screeched as he tried to slam the door shut. I had my leg in between the door and the frame so he couldn't close the door. I tried reaching Madelyne who was still wailing and howling. It was a horrific sound. All of a sudden, Tyler put me in a chokehold and dragged me from the car. I could see my dad out of the corner of my eye trying to get someone's, anyone's, attention.

"*Help!*" I screamed. "*Help me!*" But we were parked too far away from the actual police station and since it was Sunday, no one was around. "*Someone help me. Please!*"

Tyler tightened his arm around my throat. I couldn't breathe. *Oh my God*, I thought. *He's going to kill me.* Tyler was completely out of control. I knew if I didn't do something soon, I was going to blackout.

Megan Cyrulewski is an ordinary person who has faced extraordinary challenges and now wants to inspire people and show them that hope gives them the power to survive anything. *Who Am I?* is about her journey into post-partum depression, anxiety disorder, panic attacks, visits to the psych ward, divorce, domestic violence, law school, and her courageous struggle to survive with her sanity intact—and how a beautiful little girl emerged from all this chaos.

KUDOS for *Who Am I?*

Who Am I? is an honest account of one mother's failures and successes in freeing herself and her child from a destructive and abusive relationship...One thing that I learned from reading this book was that not only is verbal and emotional hurtful and wrong, it is only a short skip over the line to physical abuse. And someone who commits verbal and emotional abuse is more than likely to, eventually, resort to physical abuse when the verbal and emotional abuse no longer is enough to get what the abuser wants...It takes a lot of physical, emotional, and financial stamina to win such a case...But I think what impressed me the most was that the author appeared to be completely honest. She freely admitted her mistakes and didn't try to paint herself up as the perfect mother. – *Taylor Jones, Reviewer*

Who Am I? is a non-fiction account of a mother's struggle to protect her daughter from an abusive ex-husband...a chilling look at what can happen to a woman who gets trapped in a marriage with an abusive spouse...The book has a real ring of truth, both in the fact that the exposed her own problems, but also that she didn't try to excuse herself as being a victim of abuse. There is no "poor little me" aspect to the story, just the disappointment, despair, and outrage that a father could behave so horribly to the family he claims to love. For me, at least, the book was an eye-opener, thought-provoking, and well written—an honest account of a mother's struggle to protect her child when the man she married suddenly turns into a monster. – *Regan Murphy, Reviewer*

Who Am I?

How My Daughter Taught Me
to Let Go and Live Again

Megan Cyrulewski

A Black Opal Books Publication

Black Opal Books

BECAUSE SOME STORIES JUST HAVE TO BE TOLD

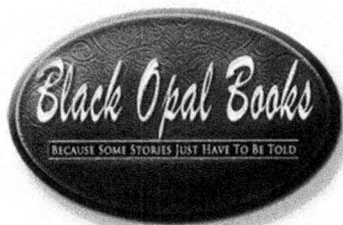

DEDICATION

To Madelyne

"A mother's love for her child is like nothing else in the world. It knows no law, no pity. It dares all things and crushes down remorselessly all that stands in its path."
– Agatha Christie

Preface

I've been crying in bed all morning. Not that unusual from any other day during the summer of 2011. I have no idea where my daughter is. My mom is probably taking care of her, again.

Good, I think to myself. She deserves better than me as her mother, anyway.

My dad is in my room, desperately trying to call my therapist.

"We're going to get you help," he tells me as he strokes my hair. "It's okay."

No, it's not. It's not okay. Nothing is okay. I am not okay. I want to die. I should die. It would be my gift to everyone. It would be my gift to myself.

My dad is talking to my therapist on the phone. "She

is upset. She keeps crying. We can't say or do anything to help calm her down."

No one can help me. I am beyond help.

I see my dad nodding as he listens to my therapist. "Okay. Okay. We're leaving right now."

I start to yell. "I don't want to go back to the hospital. I don't belong there. I can't go there again!"

My dad sits on the bed, holding my hand. "It's okay, Meggie," he repeats, using my childhood nickname. That just makes me cry even harder. I'm not Meggie anymore. I'm nobody. I'm nothing. Who am I?

Chapter 1

Ahhh... Young Love

E nvy. There is a reason why it's one of the seven deadly sins. It can kill you. It almost killed me.

The summer of 2004, I was 26 and had just gotten out of a long-term relationship. Good man, he just wasn't the right man for me.

I had just found out that my old college roommate had recently gotten engaged. The two of us were always "competing" during college: who was skinnier, who could pick up the most guys at the bar. Stupid girl stuff. Other friends of mine were either married or having babies. I think the last straw was finding out my high school sweetheart had gotten engaged. Somewhere in fantasyland, I always thought it was possible we might get back together. Needless to say, I was definitely envious.

That summer, my roommate, Jessica, bought a house. At the time we were sharing an apartment, but she asked if I wanted to move into her house. Jessica and I had known each other since high school and she was the best roommate, and one of the best friends, I have ever had. Without hesitation, I agreed. A month after moving in, we had a house warming party. That's when I met Tyler.

I knew Tyler slightly because he was engaged to one of Jessica's friends, Natalie. Tyler and Natalie and been together for about three years. They even came to a couple of parties Jessica and I had thrown at our apartment. I had never really talked to him, though.

Tyler and Natalie had broken up around the same time I had broken up with my-long term man.

Jessica didn't want to invite Tyler because she didn't want any tension between him and Natalie. A few days before the party, though, we found out Natalie was going to be out of town. Coincidentally, Tyler stopped by that same night to give something of Natalie's to Jessica. That was the first time I had really looked at him and I liked what I saw: good-looking, goofy smile, and deep-blue eyes. The attraction was instantaneous. So I decided to invite him to the house-warming party.

Why the hell not?

Natalie wasn't going to be there. After giving me the eyes of death, Jessica reluctantly told him the date and time.

The night of the party, Tyler knocked on the door. When I opened it, I gave him a hug and told him I was glad he was there because at least I had someone to flirt with. I didn't really pay much attention to him during the party. But after everyone left, Tyler and I ended up talking until five in the morning.

A couple of nights later, we went on our first date. We went to dinner and then back to his house to watch a movie. We were very open with each other. I told him about my anxiety disorder. He told me about his drug addiction and how he had been clean for years. Five months later, I moved in with him. Four months after that we got engaged, and a year later, we were married. Needless to say, the relationship was on overdrive from the beginning.

The relationship wasn't perfect, but whose is? Tyler didn't like his current job and was looking for a new one. He was trying to quit smoking because he knew I didn't like it. He was also a recovering addict and going to NA meetings. *It's a stressful time*. That became my mantra.

Tyler got angry. "It's a stressful time."

Tyler screamed at me. "It's a stressful time."

I was an independent woman in my mid-twenties, in a stable job making $55,000 a year, and climbing up the corporate ladder. I understood stress. I was also in complete denial. This was the beginning of what I would later understand was a domestic violence relationship with someone who had Narcissistic Personality Disorder (NPD). There were signs of these disorders, of course, but I didn't recognize them at the time.

My paternal family is 100% Polish. In my grandmother's generation, girls were expected to get married and have babies. A lot of babies. My grandmother was one of six children. After I graduated from high school, on every Christmas Eve, my grandmother would pray that the next year I would get married and start a family. I always smiled and told her maybe. I loved my grandmother very much. She was the only grandparent I had ever known.

After Tyler and I got engaged, we went to my grandmother's house to tell her the news she had been waiting for. When we told her, she stood up, pushed me aside, hugged Tyler, and said, "God bless you."

The memory still makes me smile. Three months later, she had a stroke. In February 2006, seven months before the wedding, my grandmother passed away. Devastation doesn't even coming close to describing how I felt. I called in sick to work, stayed in bed, and cried for two days.

The night of the funeral, my dad's company catered a dinner at my parent's house for our family. On the way to their house, I noticed that my car was low on gas. I stopped at a gas station and asked Tyler if he could pump the gas. Tyler was on the phone and told me to pump the gas myself. We were only two miles from my parents' house. I was still upset and crying from the funeral. I asked him again to please just pump the gas. He didn't even bother to answer me. I got out of the car and pumped the gas myself. When I got back into the car, I told Tyler that I was upset and a little angry. What happened next was my first glimpse into the emotional abusive side of domestic violence.

"You are such a spoiled little bitch who expects the world to be handed to you," Tyler screamed at me. "Turn the fucking car around."

Not saying a word, I turned the car around and headed back home to drop off Tyler, who kept spewing vile words.

"You and your family think you're so much better than me. Did Daddy pump your gas for you all the time? Well guess what? You actually have to do things for yourself now. It's time for you to grow up and live in the real world."

Tears streamed from my eyes. I still had not said a word.

"Your grandmother probably killed herself because she didn't want to deal with you anymore. She probably got tired of your spoiled behavior and decided death was better than you. I'm glad I'm going home because I don't want to watch your fucking family cry all night."

When we got back home, I parked in the driveway and finally let loose.

"How dare you!" I screamed at the top of my lungs. "I just lost my grandmother! Get out of my car! Get out!"

Tyler started laughing. "Look at you. You're a joke. You should get some help for those anger issues of yours. Don't bother coming back, bitch. Your shit will be on the curb."

I left and went to my parents' house. When my dad asked about Tyler, I said we got into an argument and he was at home.

My dad, who was the family peacemaker, and almost never said anything negative, muttered under his breath, "What a night for him to pick a fight."

About an hour into dinner, Tyler called me. He said he wanted to come over and apologize. At this point, I was so emotionally drained I really didn't care. When he arrived, he waltzed right into the house like nothing had ever happened. He pulled me aside and told me that he blew up because he was under so much stress from taking care of me the last couple of days. Looking back at the moment, I wonder how he even had the audacity to blame my grandmother's death for his behavior. At the time, I was just glad he wasn't mad anymore.

The next couple of months were calm. No arguments

and Tyler and I were having fun planning the wedding. Obviously, the argument the night of my grandmother's funeral was a result of stress. We got through it and according to Tyler, it wouldn't happen again.

Early June 2006, I was in bed, reading and waiting for Tyler to come home from a Narcotics Anonymous (NA) meeting. When he got home, he came upstairs and walked toward the bed. He stopped and asked if I smelled anything.

"No," I said, a little confused.

"It smells like cat piss." (We had a cat that sometimes urinated outside the litter box.)

Tyler looked around the room and picked up a bed pillow off the floor. He smelled it.

"She pissed on this pillow."

I laughed. "It's sad when the pillow is right next to me and I can't smell the pee."

Tyler didn't laugh. "Clean it up."

"I'll put it in the wash tomorrow. Just throw it in the basement."

Tyler picked up the pillow. "Bitch. You waited until I came home because you knew I would fucking clean it." He ripped the book I was reading right out of my hands and threw it across the room. "Get off your fat lazy ass, get some paper towels, and clean it!"

I started to shake. The monster had emerged again. I couldn't say anything.

Tyler picked up the pillow and shoved it in my face. "Smell it!" he screamed. "Can you smell it now, bitch? Now your face smells like cat piss. You're disgusting. Who would want you, anyway?"

Tyler threw the pillow back on the floor and stormed downstairs. I just sat in bed, paralyzed from fear. I couldn't think. I couldn't speak. I couldn't even cry.

I don't know how much time had passed before Tyler came back. Without saying a word, he picked up two water bottles I had sitting on the nightstand beside me, unscrewed the tops, and poured water on me. He laughed and went back downstairs.

I took off my pajamas, turned out the light, and rolled to the dry side of the bed. Before long, I heard Tyler come up the stairs again. I began to shake. He ripped the covers off of me.

"You would sleep in a wet bed. I should have poured cat piss on you and let you sleep in that." He laughed. "Get out of my fucking bed and sleep outside."

I got out of bed and put on dry pajamas. I took off my engagement ring, threw it on the bed, and left. I went to Jessica's house and asked if I could spend the night. I didn't talk about what happened. I just told her that the engagement was off and I just needed to sleep. Jessica never asked any questions and I loved her for that.

Before long, my phone rang and it was Tyler. He asked me to come back home. I was hesitant, but he convinced me to come back home and talk. I left Jessica a note and went back home.

When I got home, Tyler was sitting on the couch. "I'm going to get a six-pack of beer, drink it, and kill myself."

Shocked, I sat down next to him. "Do you want me to call someone? Should I call your sponsor? I don't know what to do."

Tyler kept repeating. "I'm going to kill myself." He was crying, but there weren't any tears.

I hugged him. "We'll get through this. We'll get help. Please don't kill yourself. I love you too much."

"Thank you," Tyler smiled. And just like that, he got up, told me he loved me, and went to bed.

Looking back, I now realize that this was Tyler's way of manipulation. He knew he let his anger get out of control, to the point that I walked away. To get me back, he subtly blamed me for what happened by alluding that he was going to commit suicide. At the time, I felt guilty for not cleaning the damn pillow. If I had cleaned that pillow, this never would have happened. I promised myself to be more careful in the future.

The next morning, my engagement ring was on my nightstand.

Chapter 2

Stuck

Unlike most girls, I had never imagined a "dream wedding." I never played bride or even had a dress-up wedding gown. I was always cynical of women who seemed to spend so much time planning their wedding instead of focusing on the marriage. With that being said, I absolutely loved my wedding.

I love American History, especially the Civil War era. While other girls had crushes on boys, I dreamed of what it would have been like if I had lived in the 1800s and married Abraham Lincoln. I even dressed as Abraham Lincoln for a sixth-grade play. So when I got engaged, I knew I wanted to get married at Greenfield Village, part of The Henry Ford Museum in Dearborn, a suburb of Detroit.

The wedding was beautiful. We were married in a chapel on the grounds of Greenfield Village. Our reception was in a tavern from the 1800s. I missed my grandmother immensely, but I lit a candle at the service in her memory. We only had 4 out of the 135 people that we invited that couldn't make it. Our guests were extremely generous in gifting us with approximately $6,000. We agreed to spend about $1,000 on our honeymoon in Puerto Vallarta and put the rest in our savings.

Tyler and I had to delay our honeymoon for a few weeks after the wedding because of responsibilities at my work. The morning of our honeymoon, we needed to stop at the bank to withdrawal some cash for airport parking. I handed the withdrawal slip to the teller.

"You show a negative balance in your account," said the teller.

I was shocked. "That's not possible. We just deposited $6,000 a couple of weeks ago."

"You have a negative balance of $324." I could tell the teller was embarrassed.

I turned to Tyler. "We need to go home and call the corporate office or something. How could they lose $6,000?"

As we drove home, Tyler dropped a bomb. "I paid my bills with the money."

"What?"

"I was behind in some of my bills and I must have not calculated right."

I was fuming. "What bills? What the hell are you talking about?"

That's how I found out that Tyler had over $60,000 worth of debt and I'd had no clue.

When we got home, I couldn't even look at him I was so angry. We had three hours to catch our flight and we didn't have any money.

I sat on the couch crying. Meanwhile, Tyler gathered up all the loose change we had around the house. That was his solution to our problem. Cash in loose change.

When he left to go scrounge up whatever money he could find, I called my parents.

"Mom! We have no money!" I was hysterical.

My mom, clearly confused, told me to calm down.

"We went to the bank and we have no money. Tyler used all of our wedding money to pay his bills." I was so embarrassed to even have to call my parents.

"It's okay, honey. Your dad and I will fix this and we can talk when you two get home. Is $1,000 okay?"

Was it okay? Not even close. I was grateful to my parents, of course, but they never should have been put into that position of having to bail us out.

I wiped the tears from my face. "Thanks, Mom. I'm so sorry."

"Don't worry about it. I'll send your dad to the bank and have him deposit it into your account," my mom said. "Are you going to be okay?"

I heard Tyler pull up in the driveway. I had a decision to make. Either I could continue to be angry and not go on our honeymoon, or I could agree to set the problem aside and try to have a good time. I chose the latter. I thanked my mom profusely and promised to call when we got to Houston (our overnight layover before Mexico).

Tyler walked into the house. "I cashed in our change and we have a little over $300!" He was like a little boy. I was disgusted. We were supposed to have a little over $6,000 in our bank account and he was excited because he was able to get $300?

"My parents are giving us $1,000 for our honeymoon. So let's just go."

"Great!" Tyler exclaimed.

On our way to the airport, my mom called to make sure I was okay. Tyler answered my phone because I was driving.

"She's fine," Tyler, answered my mom. "Do you want to talk to her?" He handed the phone to me.

"Are you okay?" my mom asked.

"I'm fine," I said. "Thank you again for helping out."

"Just try to have a good time, okay?"

That became my mantra for the honeymoon and I

was actually able to put it aside. We both were able to have a wonderful, relaxing vacation in beautiful Puerto Vallarta. Our honeymoon is one of the fondest memories I have from our marriage. We spent days swimming in the pool and frolicking in the waves, like children without a care in the world. We danced in the town square to a Mexican band that played Neil Diamond's, "Sweet Caroline." Tyler indulged me when I insisted we take a tour of Elizabeth Taylor and Richard Burton's love nest. We bargained in the markets for keepsakes. I hated the thought of going back to reality.

People say the honeymoon phase of a marriage usually ends after the first year. Our honeymoon phase ended when the honeymoon ended. I decided not to discuss the wedding money. My thought was that we couldn't move forward in our marriage if I brought up the past.

I was very fortunate to have a good job that paid very well. I worked in the non-profit sector. Starting with my first job right out of college, I worked extremely hard to move up in my career. By the time I was 27, I was an Associate Director of Development and my salary was $55,000 per year.

On the other hand, Tyler couldn't have cared less about work. He dropped out of high school in the eleventh grade. He did get his GED when he was 22, but he had absolutely no goals in life. He worked in sales and if he worked to his full potential, we would have been millionaires. He had the ability to talk anyone into anything. (I married him, didn't I?) The problem was that Tyler was extremely lazy. He didn't have to report to an office or his supervisor every day because he was allowed to work from home.

I called home from work one day to let him know I had to stay late. It was 1:00 in the afternoon and he was still in bed. That was how our finances worked, too. I made the money and he spent it. Why pay bills when he could buy anything he wanted? I let it go on—until he stole my work bonus and bought a guitar. I was livid.

"That money was supposed to go into savings!" I screamed at him. "I am not going to keep working my ass off so you can lay in bed all day and then buy toys for yourself!"

"I'm depressed," he whined.

"Depressed? Are you fucking kidding me right now? You don't do a damn thing!" I gave him an ultimatum, my first of many. "You need to get your ass out of bed and work. You also need to get a second job to start paying off your debt. I will *not* support both of us when you are able to work."

I left that night and stayed at a hotel. I knew if I stayed home the argument would have escalated and I just didn't have the energy. I had serious doubts about our marriage, and we had only been married for two months. I dreaded going home after work the next day.

To my surprise, Tyler had had what I like to call his "Come to Jesus" moment. (Again, one of many.) He sat me down and went through his new "life plan." He was going to get up in the morning the same time I did and start his workday. He was able to get a second job, delivering pizzas three nights a week. This new life plan worked for about two weeks. While Tyler did stick with his new work schedule, he spent the money he made from his second job instead of paying off his debt.

I had confided our financial difficulties to my parents. I didn't ask for money, I just wanted advice. My parents offered a solution. Since my grandmother's death, our family had been fixing up her house in order to put it on the market. However, it was around this time that the real estate bubble burst and we were having a lot of trouble finding a buyer. The house was jointly owned by my father and my aunt and had been paid off for a while. My parents offered to buy out my aunt's half and let Tyler and I live in the house for free. The opportunity would allow us to pay off Tyler's debt and save some money. I had also been thinking about quitting my job and going to law school. (Trying to fundraise and ask people for money during a recession wasn't fun.)

Tyler was ecstatic. We worked out a new life plan. We would move into my grandmother's house and rent out our current house. I also decided to take the LSAT (the exam for law school admission). If I scored well enough, I would apply to law school, hopefully get accepted, and quit my job. Tyler would keep working both of his jobs, pay off his debt, and save money.

We moved in May 2007. I took the LSAT, applied to law schools, and was accepted! I chose Thomas M. Cooley Law School because I didn't have to wait until September 2008 to start my classes. Instead, I could start classes in January 2008. I quit my job, took out one of *many* student loans, bought my textbooks, and spent the next few months preparing to go back to school. Everything seemed like it was finally falling into place. But, of course, it wouldn't last.

The week before I was to begin school, Tyler explained our new life plan. "I'm going to file for bankruptcy."

Shocked, I was barely able to stutter, "What?"

Tyler explained. "We just have too much debt."

"What about the other house? I thought we were going to rent it out?"

"I'm just going to let it go."

"Why? Why don't we rent it out and then see what happens? Bankruptcy seems too drastic."

Tyler had his mind made up and no one was going to change it. "This is what I'm doing. If you don't like it, then you can fuck off."

Talk about overload. I started law school in a week and now I had to research bankruptcy laws because, God forbid, that Tyler should have to do that himself. My main concern was that, because we were married, I didn't want to have to file bankruptcy as well, because then, both of our credit ratings would be screwed.

We were able to find a bankruptcy attorney and I insisted on going with Tyler to the first meeting. The attorney was extremely helpful. Under the law, I didn't have to be included in the bankruptcy filing. However, I still felt that filing for bankruptcy was extreme. While Tyler was ready to sign the paperwork right then, I told the attorney that we needed some time to talk it over. Bad idea.

As soon as we got home, Tyler exploded. "You think you are so much better than everyone else, don't you?" Then he mocked me. "I'm Megan and my parents have done everything for me. I'm a spoiled rich bitch who has no idea what happens in the real world."

"I think that you are lazy and are looking for the easy way out!" All of the built-up frustration about the bankruptcy finally spilled out of me. "This is typical Tyler. When things get too hard, you have to find someone to save you, once again. Why take the responsibility to fix your debt when you can wipe it out with bankruptcy?"

"Maybe if you had not decided to quit because work was just too fucking difficult for you, we wouldn't be in this situation," Tyler shot back.

Once again, everything was my fault. I entered our marriage without *any* debt, yet Tyler's debt now became my problem because, God forbid, Tyler *ever* take responsibility for his own actions. Apparently, even though I quit my job to go back to school to better our future, this was not good enough for him. And clearly the fact that my parents paid my aunt $60,000 of their own money so that we could live in my grandmother's house for free was not good enough for Tyler.

We were only a year into our marriage and I knew it was not going to work. I wasn't in love with Tyler anymore.

Chapter 3

I Am a Walking Cliché

I was a completely different person before I met Tyler. I was outgoing, relaxed, hard to offend, and just constantly laughing. I was diagnosed with anxiety disorder when I was 19, but after learning through therapy how to cope with the panic attacks, I didn't let my disorder take over my life.

A year into our marriage, I started becoming more of an introvert. I told Tyler it was because of the stress from law school. However, the real reason was much deeper. I lived in constant fear of my husband every day. The physical abuse was minimal. The emotional abuse was what tore me down. I had never known such emptiness.

Tyler loved to tell me that the only reason he married me was because no one else would. He also told me that the only reason I had friends was because they felt sorry for me. He used to call me a "joke" on a weekly basis. For example, if I expressed an opinion that was contrary to his, I was a joke. If I went to bed early because I was tired, I was a joke. If one of my friends cancelled plans, I was a joke.

My world revolved around figuring out what type of mood Tyler was in every second of every day. My biggest fear was that I never knew what would set Tyler off into one of his tantrums. If he had a bad day at work, I would bear the brunt of that day. If I asked him to do the dishes and he didn't feel like it, he would scream at me to get off my lazy ass and do them myself.

I had no idea that this was not how a marriage worked. Growing up, I never saw my parents argue, but I attributed that to the fact that my dad hated any type of conflict. (My dad and I avoid conflict like the plague.) The only other serious relationship I ever had was with my high school sweetheart and he treated me like a princess. However, we were only seventeen.

It was at this point in my marriage that I decided not to confide in anyone about the abuse. I was completely embarrassed because I knew that it wasn't normal but I didn't want confirmation from anyone. I didn't want someone to say to me that this wasn't normal. I also didn't want to admit that I had made a mistake in marrying Tyler.

He knew that he had an anger problem and he would feel sorry after he yelled at me. I would usually come home and find a sappy card and my favorite candy on my pillow as his way of an apology. However, even that was a double-edged sword because if I didn't acknowledge the gifts, he would call me an ungrateful bitch.

Tyler also loved to dole out punishments as a form of abuse. There were times he would give me the silent treatment. He wouldn't talk to me for days. He acted as though I didn't even exist. Also, Tyler knew that some things really bothered me, and he would use those things against me. For example, he knew that I hated dirty dishes in the sink, so he wouldn't wash them. Or he wouldn't clean up after himself, which was also one of my pet peeves.

The worst punishment was when he used my anxiety against me. I have panic attacks if I feel like I am trapped, going to be sick in public, driving fast, or driving in bad weather. The last was because I was in a horrific car accident during a rainstorm. If we were in the car having an argument, Tyler would deliberately drive faster, knowing that would cause a panic attack.

Law school was my escape. I made new friends and was thankful every day when I had class. I didn't confide in anyone about my marriage. I just let everyone think I had this great marriage. I really didn't even talk about Tyler that much at school because when I walked through the school doors, I left him behind.

The first year of law school was extremely hard. Under-graduate school was *nothing* compared to law school. I knew that law school was going to be a challenge for me because I was not good at exams and law school grades are based on an exam at the end of each term

By the end of the first year, I was seriously thinking of dropping out. My grades weren't stellar. In fact, I was barely above academic probation. I ended up taking a semester off to decide what I wanted to do. I knew I didn't want to work in the non-profit sector again, but I didn't have experience anywhere else. My academic advisor was my saving grace. She told me not to give up. She said that if I loved going to school and enjoyed learning the law, then I needed to stick it out. I knew that if I wanted to make it work, I was going to have to work a lot harder than most.

I decided to give law school another chance and it was one of the best decisions of my life. My grades improved immediately. I still wasn't getting a 4.0, but at least I was not close to academic probation anymore.

I had just settled into my second year of law school when Tyler decided it was time to have a baby. I was a little shocked, but not surprised. Tyler's best friend recently had an adorable little baby girl. Tyler always wanted what everyone else had. Not only that, but he wanted to be better than everyone else. So when his friend had a baby, that's when Tyler wanted a baby, too. When Tyler brought it up, I was excited until I took the time to really think it through. I knew having a baby was something I didn't want to do.

My family and friends knew that I didn't want kids. This decision had nothing to do with my childhood. I had a wonderful childhood. I just never felt maternal. I didn't like being around kids. I had no desire to have kids. I never even played house with my friends growing up. I was also focused on my career. Tyler and I had talked about children before we got married and we both agreed that having a family was not the life we wanted. We both wanted to travel and have the freedom to do whatever we wanted whenever we wanted.

A few days after Tyler had broached the subject of a baby, I drove out to my parents' home and asked my mom for advice. While I was explaining Tyler's reasoning to my mom, I had a full-on panic attack. Obviously, I knew that I was not ready to have a child. However, the panic attack was not brought on by the idea of having a baby. I was afraid because I was scared to tell Tyler about my decision.

I remember shaking uncontrollably driving back home from my parent's house. When Tyler came home, I was lying in bed. He made a joke about how I was practicing "being pregnant" because I was in bed in the middle of the day. When I didn't laugh, he knew something was going on.

"I can't do this right now. I just can't have a baby." I started to explain my reasons, but he cut me off.

Sure enough, he was pissed. He yelled vile, hateful things to me. He said he shouldn't have married me. I was selfish, not giving him what he wanted. I should be lucky that he even wanted to have sex with me because I was so fat.

He stalked out of the room as I cried. I know he heard me. It took him a couple of days to calm down. He gave me the silent treatment. During that time, I really thought he was going to divorce me and find someone who wanted to have kids.

Even though I was upset, I think I surprised Tyler because that was the first time I had really stood my ground and I wasn't backing down from my decision. When Tyler decided that my punishment had gone on long enough, he actually wanted to hear how I felt. I told him that we should revisit the idea in a year and maybe I would feel differently. I felt that I needed to be farther along in my school and Tyler needed to have a better job. He made a decent salary but part of his salary was based on commission and the country was in the middle of the recession.

I also told Tyler that he needed to work on his anger

problems. I was adamant that we would not bring a child into this world if he continued having anger issues. He completely agreed but I knew he was placating me. He never had any intention on trying to help himself.

We really didn't talk about a baby after that discussion until one of my close friends found out she was pregnant. And this time, I had baby envy. So one night in February 2010, I told Tyler I wanted a baby. He was shocked because we really hadn't talked about it in a long time, but once I put the idea out there, he was off and running. He really talked me into it. I look back on that conversation and realize he played me very well. He talked about how he wanted to be a good father and wanted his child to have a better childhood than he did. Basically, he told me everything I wanted to hear.

In retrospect, a baby was a bad idea. Our marriage was in trouble. The emotional abuse was getting worse. Tyler quit his old job because we were scraping by—barely—on his salary. He started a new job, but he hated it because it was manual labor. He was taking his anger out on me every chance he could. He stopped going to NA meetings and when he didn't go to meetings, it was only a matter of time before he had another anger episode. I had also started a really great, but extremely busy, internship at the Federal Immigration Court in Detroit.

The bottom line, which I can admit now, was that I agreed to have a baby because I wanted to save our marriage. I read about women who started a family for this reason and thought how could anyone be so stupid? But the way Tyler talked and the excitement he portrayed really convinced me that a baby was the saving grace we needed.

I talked to my gynecologist about trying to have a baby. She said that it usually takes a woman an average of six months to get pregnant. It takes even longer if the woman is on birth control. I thought the timing was perfect. I figured we had about six months to get used to idea of having a baby. Also, we planned a trip to Bahamas in April 2010. We both thought that would be the perfect place to conceive a child, but why not have some fun before the trip? So, I stopped my birth control in February.

I got pregnant on the first try.

Chapter 4

And Baby Makes Three...No, Just Two

To say both of us were in shock when we found out I was pregnant might be the understatement of the century. However, I kind of had a feeling I was pregnant. My friends who had already had children said they knew when they were pregnant, even before the pregnancy test confirmation. Some people might be skeptical, but after experiencing pregnancy, I absolutely believe a woman knows when she is pregnant. My body felt different. I kept trying to tell Tyler that something felt different, but he didn't want to believe me. But I knew. I bought a bunch of early pregnancy detection tests that are only sold online. I didn't have the patience to wait for an over-the-counter test to prove what I already knew. Sure enough, one night when Tyler was home, I took the test and it came out positive. Tyler was in such disbelief, he thought the test was defective. He actually took a pregnancy test himself to prove to me that the testing strip was defective. When his came back negative—surprise— he finally had to admit I was pregnant.

When reality set in, we were happy. I wanted to tell my parents immediately. I honestly didn't know how my mom was going to react because the last time I'd talked to her to about a baby, I'd had a panic attack. It was early evening, but we decided to go to my parents' house. We called on the way there and made up a story about wanting to drop off an early Easter gift (Easter was two weeks away). When we called, she said my dad wasn't home but to come over anyway. We stopped at Hallmark on the way. I wanted to get a "Surprise, we're expecting" card. Tyler and I were giddy when we gave her the card.

She opened it, read it, and said, "You're kidding." Straight face. Not a shred of happiness.

"Surprise!" I yelled.

"You're kidding," she repeated.

"No. Tyler didn't believe it either until he took his own pregnancy test." I laughed nervously. This was not turning out well at all.

"Well." She sighed. "I don't know what you want me to say."

"When is dad coming home?" I asked.

"Not for a while." She put the card back in the envelope. "I think you should let me tell him."

Tyler tugged my arm. "We should probably go."

I nodded. I couldn't speak. On the way home, I was devastated. I was mad, confused, sobbing uncontrollably, speechless and just…hurt. Tyler didn't say a word on the way home. I knew he was upset. He was probably more upset with me for letting my mom's opinion control my own emotions.

(On a side note, as for my mother's reaction when we told her I was pregnant, my mom and I talked about her reaction years later. She explained that she was shocked and concerned because she knew I didn't want to have kids. Also, she didn't want me to quit law school, especially when I was about two-thirds of the way finished.)

When Tyler and I got back home we just sat in the living room like two kids with their hands caught in the cookie jar.

What the hell did we just do? Getting pregnant seemed like a good idea, but when it happened so quickly, reality set in and it wasn't good. We sat in our living room in silence.

I had to break the ice. "What should we do?"

He looked at me. "What do you mean?"

"Should we get rid of it?"

Tyler was shocked. "Are you talking about an abortion?

I shrugged my shoulders. "Maybe we're not ready."

Tyler was *very* adamant against it. "That's *my* baby! How *dare* you even think of getting rid of it! I will take you to court and sue your ass and show everybody what a selfish bitch you really are!"

As I let those words sink in, I think that was the first (and only) time his outburst was good for me. It kind of shocked me into reality. In all honesty, because of my Catholic upbringing, I would not have been able to have an abortion. And obviously now, I thank Tyler for making the decision for both of us.

In fact, a few days after I found out I was pregnant, I started bleeding and was scared I had miscarried. I immediately went to my gynecologist for a blood test. When she called the next day to let me know my levels were normal, I cried with relief. That's when I knew this pregnancy was meant to happen.

The pregnancy definitely happened at a very busy time for me. I was just finishing up my federal court immigration internship and had secured another internship in a prosecutor's office, working with special victims. These two internships were vastly different from each other and I learned more valuable information from both than I had learned in any classroom.

During my federal immigration internship, I drafted

memos to the immigration judges on why an immigrant who was seeking asylum should or should not be deported. While I am certainly not going to discuss my political views on immigration law, I will say that the experience helped me learn how to properly research the law and draft legal documents.

My prosecutor internship, on the other hand, was by far the best internship (or job) I have ever had. The people I worked with were some of the most dedicated individuals committed to justice that I have ever had the privilege of working with, and I aspire to be like them one day in my own legal career.

My doctor told me since I was busy with my internship and a full course load, she wanted me to rest as much as possible. I didn't want to tell anyone I was pregnant until after the first trimester. I wanted to make sure that we got through the first trimester before sharing the news. Tyler couldn't keep his mouth shut. He told everyone he knew—his friends, his boss, a customer who couldn't even speak English—that I was pregnant. Then he posted the news on the mother of all social media: Facebook. Soon enough I was receiving private messages: "Is Tyler joking?" or "What is going on?" My personal favorite from one of my closest friends, "Why am I learning about this on FB, bitch?" ("Bitch" turned out to an endearing, yet pissed off, term.)

So, I told all my friends and posted it on my Facebook page. My friends' reaction was the same as my mom. No one really took me seriously until I posted the picture of the damn sonogram. My closest friends were happy, but not happy. Basically what I heard from them was, "If you are happy, then we will support you."

To get away from some of the drama, Tyler and I went to the Bahamas for a mini-vacation. We booked it before we found out I was pregnant, but we got the "Okay" from my doctor that I could go and enjoy. When I posted on Facebook that Tyler and I were going to the Bahamas, the majority of the responses were, "Have fun because it's the last time you will ever be free!" (Really? Because I thought I could keep traveling and do whatever I wanted once the baby was born.)

I have to admit that the trip to the Bahamas was one of the best vacations I've ever been on. Tyler and I milked the pregnancy big time. (We had no shame.) The airline staff was very accommodating with extra pillows and snacks, our hotel room was upgraded, and we got a lot of free desserts. We stayed at The Atlantis, which is absolutely gorgeous. For four days, we never left the island. It was the perfect "baby moon."

Once we got back home, Tyler wanted to call his mother, Lucy to tell her about the pregnancy. The relationship between Tyler and Lucy had been extremely complicated almost from birth. Tyler's parents divorced when he was little and it was not an amicable divorce.

His parents had joint custody of Tyler and his brother, Ben. Both Tyler's parents remarried and while Tyler got along with his various stepmothers, he clashed with his stepfather all the time. Tyler and Ben grew up during a heated custody battle. While Ben stayed out of trouble, Tyler was out of control.

I can't say much about Tyler's childhood because all I heard were his recollection of events, and now I really don't know how much was true. I never talked to Lucy about his childhood and I don't think it's fair for me to speculate what happened. I do know that when Tyler was thirteen, Lucy made the decision to send Tyler to a juvenile detention center because he was completely out of control. When Tyler's father heard about this, he agreed to let Tyler live with him and forego the joint custody arrangement. Tyler's brother Ben stayed with Lucy and her husband. From that point on, it was evident that sides had formed within the family: Tyler and his dad against Ben and his mom. That dynamic continues to this day.

During the years, Tyler and his mother went through bouts of civility, however, when I found out I was pregnant; Tyler and Lucy hadn't talked in over a year. I tried to convince Tyler not to expect anything from his mom, but he thought that once she heard I was pregnant, she would want to be a part of his life again. He tried calling and e-mailing, but never heard back.

Toward the end of my first trimester, Tyler received

an invitation to a barbeque from his aunt (Lucy's sister). Tyler called his aunt and she thought it was a good idea if we came. She said that Lucy had always wanted a grand-child and maybe this baby would bring the family closer together. Personally, I wasn't expecting a miracle.

After a 45-minute drive, we arrived at the barbeque. A few of the cousins were in the garage and congratulat-ed us on the baby. Tyler's aunt said that Lucy was on the back patio and we should say hello. As soon as we stepped on the patio, Lucy stood up, went inside, and banged the door. Clearly, she did not want us to be there. Tyler and I looked at each other, wondering what to do. Lucy then opened the door and asked if she could talk to Tyler—alone.

I stood outside and had a very awkward conversation with the rest of the family. We were trying to keep things light but with the yelling and swearing in the background, it just wasn't working out very well. Finally, Tyler came to the door and told me we were leaving. As we left, Ty-ler screamed at his mom.

"You were never a real mom," Tyler yelled. "Go back inside and act like you're the victim, bitch. Fuck you."

Shocked, and a little embarrassed, I hurried to the car. As we drove away, I asked Tyler what happened. Lucy had confronted him and spewed the words I felt like she had been waiting to say for years:

"I don't want you in my life. Don't ever contact me. I don't care that you are having a baby. I'm done."

Done with Tyler. Done with me. Done with any relationship. She was done.

Tyler cried on the way home. It was the first time I had seen real, genuine tears. This was one of the few times I honestly felt bad for him. That didn't last long.

That barbeque was the turning point in the pregnancy. After that, Tyler definitely stepped back from it. It seemed as though because his mom didn't welcome the baby with open arms and was done with us, Tyler was done with the pregnancy. All support from Tyler was gone.

If I asked him to run up to the store to get me something, he never did. If I asked him to rub my swollen feet, he never did. If I asked him to rub my back, he never did. I learned to never ask him for anything.

Even though Tyler did not care about the pregnancy anymore, he sure put on a good show in public.

"How are you feeling, hon?"

"Put your feet on my lap and I'll rub them."

"Do you need anything to drink?"

I think this was the first time in my life I wanted to go out more than stay home.

As the weeks got closer to finding out the gender of the baby, everyone was excited, even Tyler.

I wanted a little girl. I wanted to buy pink frilly outfits. I wanted her to take dance lessons just like I did. I also played sports, so she was definitely going to be a future athlete. Most importantly, I already had a name picked out: Madelyne Rose. Rose was my grandmother's name.

On the day of the appointment, I could barely breathe. After waiting almost an hour, my name was called. I lay on the table, pulled up my shirt, and was ready to roll.

"Oh, someone's in a hurry," the technician said with a laugh.

I'm not trying to be stereotypical, but our technician was a very gay man. (Think Cam from Modern Family.) So imagine the following conversation knowing that information:

"Do you want to know the gender?"

"YES!" I exclaimed. Wasn't it obvious?

"Well, my my. We need to just find out who is dancing in that belly of yours." He reached for a bottle. "A little warm gel. A dab will do ya!" (Note to all future mothers, a "little" means half the bottle so bring a change of clothes.)

"Hmmm...yes. Here's the head," the technician said as he kept moving his little ultrasound wand around my stomach. "Here's the spinal cord. The heart looks great."

Holy shit, just tell us the Goddamn sex.

"Well, well, well!" he squealed. "Now are you sure

you want to find out the gender because I can tell you right now. I see that little cutie in there!"

Smiling while wanting to punch him in the face, I asked, "What is that cutie in there?"

He took a dramatic breath, "It's—a—*girl*!"

I cried. The poor technician thought I was upset.

"Now, now, dear."

Tyler interjected. "We wanted a girl."

"Oh well! My work here is done!"

I think the technician was on the verge of tears. As soon as we found out the gender, we told everyone right away. Tyler wanted to tell his mother even though I tried desperately to talk him out of it, knowing it would just cause more pain.

"Tyler, she said she didn't care that we were having a baby. Just let it go."

"My aunt said my mom always wanted a girl. When she didn't have any girls, then she told everyone she wanted a granddaughter."

I let it go. It seemed to me that Tyler was just setting himself up for another disappointment.

Once we knew it was a girl, my mom started planning the baby shower. My mom went above and beyond anything I could have imagined. Knowing how much I love American History, my mom booked the shower at Meadowbrook Hall, a historic mansion built by the automotive pioneers, the Dodge family.

The shower was amazing. Guests were invited on a tour of the historic home while the brunch was being prepared. Everyone kept complimenting my mom on a beautiful shower. Everyone from my side came: my friends, family, my dad's relatives, and my mom's girlfriends of over forty years. Invitations were sent to Tyler's side of the family. We did get gifts from his relatives but did not hear anything from his mom. We reserved an entire table for Tyler's mom's side of the family, but no one showed up. Thank God people were too polite to ask questions. However, because his mom did not come to the shower, Tyler sulked like a child the entire time.

When it was time to open gifts, my best friend, Alison, and her daughter, Jenn, helped me. Tyler sat on his ass during the entire shower. I gave a quick speech, thanking everyone for coming and for their generosity. I especially thanked my parents for being the best role models any child would be lucky to follow. I cried when I told everyone Madelyne Rose was named after my Grandmother.

Tyler didn't thank anyone. He didn't stand up and thank people for gifts. He didn't help open the gifts. I was on my feet the entire time, opening gifts and handing out prizes. Tyler didn't care. After about an hour, I leaned into his ear and pleaded with him to stand so I could sit. He didn't even answer me.

After the shower was over, my parents and I thanked

everyone. Tyler was MIA again. My dad, Alison, Jenn, and myself and even some of the wait staff helped load our car with the gifts. Tyler finally showed up when everything was loaded.

When we got home, Tyler was pissed that I wasn't going to help unload the car.

"You are so fucking lazy. What's the matter with you?" he screamed at me.

"I've been on my feet for the last three hours. I'm tired. I just want to take a hot bath. Can't you unload the stuff yourself?" I was crying at this point.

"Fine. Don't unload anything. But don't expect me to do it."

"We can't keep everything in the car!"

Tyler looked smug. "I guess you're going to have to move your fat lazy ass and help."

I was tired but I carried our gifts inside because Tyler didn't want to do it by himself. I sat in the rocking chair in the nursery and just looked at everything again. I was so incredibly thankful. I called Tyler to come look at all the gifts. He didn't answer me. I could hear the TV in the background. After he brought the rest of the gifts into the nursery, he never looked at them again.

When I went to bed that night, I had the worst leg cramps I have ever had from standing up for such a long time that day. I was crying in pain throughout the night while Tyler snored soundly.

After the shower, Tyler became even more with-
drawn because he was no longer the center of attention.
When we were in public, he didn't even bother putting on
a show anymore. When the diaper-changing table arrived,
he watched me struggle to put it together while he sat on
the couch, eating McDonald's. When I asked him to help
me hang up a couple of pictures in the nursery, he said he
was too busy. He was done.

I still attended law school throughout the entire
pregnancy. I had to take at least six credits to be eligible
for financial aid, so I chose two classes that required a
final paper not an exam since my due date was close to
exam week. I thought the timing of the birth was perfect
because I would have a month off between semesters.
Obviously, I had absolutely no experience with babies.

Toward the end of the pregnancy, the strain on my
body felt awful. Madelyne was over eight pounds and
still growing. At that point in the pregnancy, I was tired,
stressed, hurting, and just wanted the baby out. Tyler
didn't care. At one point, I told Tyler that I couldn't help
with the household chores anymore and asked if he could
wash the dishes and vacuum. That was a mistake. If I
asked Tyler to do something, he made it a point not do
anything. So when the dishes piled up, I did them. When
the cat fur clumps accumulated on the carpet, I vacu-
umed.

The last week of November, I started getting Braxton-hicks contractions. One afternoon, I thought I was in labor and called Tyler. He told me he was busy working and to drive myself to the hospital but to call him back if I was admitted. It was a false alarm so I was sent home.

On December first, I started having contractions again. I called my doctor and she said go to hospital. Thankfully this was at night so Tyler was at home. When we got to triage, I was only one and one half centimeters dilated so my doctor didn't want to induce.

The nurses told me to walk around the hospital for two hours to try to get something happening. I hated every second of those two hours, but on the positive side, I knew where everything was located in the hospital for future reference.

After our walk, we went back to triage but nothing had changed. (Madelyne was already showing her stubborn side.) My doctor told the nurses to admit me and start Pitocin. I was ecstatic. Finally this baby was coming out! That euphoria lasted until the Pitocin kicked in.

Pitocin is the dirty little secret of labor that no one wants to talk about. The nurses call it the "devil's juice."

For those who have never had the pleasure of Pitocin running through your veins, let me try to explain it with this analogy: You're in your happy place, on the beaches of Bora Bora. You're in the sun, relaxing with a drink when all of a sudden you feel a pinch on your stomach. You look down and see a little crab that wandered out of the water to say hello. You feel happy and say, "Well, hello there, little crab."

You close your eyes and layback down, smiling. What a cute little crab. Until all of a sudden you feel a couple of pinches on your stomach. You look down and the little crab has brought a friend. Hmmm, you think to yourself. You're still in your happy place but some of that euphoria has receded. You cautiously lay back down.

Then, before you can take another sip from your umbrella drink, your cute little crab friend invited his entire family to your happy place. There are about eight hundred crabs pinching your stomach, back, legs, breasts, and just for good measure, your vagina.

But the worst part of all is that everyone is watching you scream in pain and saying, "Sorry, but you asked for it," and they walk away.

Needless to say, if someone had told me the real story of Pitocin, there was no way in the depths of Hell I would ever have agreed to be induced. The nurse who was in charge of my room was a "told-you-so" bitch. She was against medicine and was a champion for natural labor. I begged her for an epidural but she kept repeating that I wasn't dilated enough and I had a long way to go. (Note: the entire four hours I had a Pitocin IV, she never once checked to see if I had dilated.) So at four in the morning, I told her to stop the Pitocin and I was sent home.

The car ride back home was horrible. Every bump vibrated up my back, through my abdomen and seemed to cause endless contractions. When we got back home, I was crying in pain. Tyler was so scared that he called my doctor because I think at this point, even he knew something was wrong. Tyler handed the phone to me and my doctor was confused about why I left hospital. I told her the nurse didn't want to give me an epidural and if I stopped Pitocin, I had to leave.

My doctor said she was never called about my request for an epidural and she admitted she was surprised because she knew I wanted that epidural as soon as possible.

She was livid and told me to go back to the hospital. By the time Tyler drove me back to the hospital, I was six centimeters dilated. I wanted the epidural at three centimeters. My happy place was non-existent.

The hospital admitted me (to a different room with a different nurse) and paged the anesthesiologist to inject the epidural. The anesthesiologist explained the procedure and said because the injection went into the spine, the procedure was going to hurt. Wow, really? Because up until this point, labor was the best experience of my life!

As if not getting the epidural until this point in my labor wasn't bad enough, the anesthesiologist had trouble getting the needle into the injection site in my back. It took two anesthesiologists, two nurses, and an hour to get the damn drug into my spinal cord.

My parents and Tyler's dad and step-mom arrived at the hospital soon after the epidural ordeal. Before they came into the room, my nurse told me to page her if I had any problems or if I wanted anyone to leave. Between my painful contractions and my epidural moment, my nurse and I bonded and I told her that Tyler's dad was an ass-hole and I really didn't want him at the hospital. She had my back.

After a couple of more hours, I finally felt like I needed to push. I had Tyler tell everyone to leave. My parents and Tyler's step-mom completely understood. Tyler's dad wanted to stay. Even Tyler was fed up with his dad at the point and told him to get the hell out of the room.

My nurse came in and explained how to push. Basically it felt like I was going to have a bowel movement and I needed to push. Also a little tidbit that's a secret that no one wants to share—while you are pushing, you are pretty likely to have a bowel movement right there in front of your nurse, significant other, doctor, and any in-terns along for the ride.

I pushed for over an hour and Madelyne did not move at all. Halfway through pushing, I needed the oxy-gen mask because I almost passed out. When it was clear to me that I had absolutely no energy left to push, I asked for a C-section. The nurse wanted to try again and my doctor said to try at least another15 more minutes. I usually find myself to be a very accommodating person, however, I screamed to no one in particular, "NO ONE IS FUCKING LISTENING TO ME."

There was a moment of silence. Tyler, my doctor, and the nurse looked at each other and then sprang into action. I wasn't fooling around anymore. Get. This. Kid. Out.

As they wheeled me into the operating room, my nurse told me not to feel guilty about not having a natural birth because most of the nurses got C-sections. Apparently they had seen the trauma and pain of natural or vaginal birth and did not wish that upon themselves.

When everything was set up in the operating room, one of the nurses asked if I wanted a mirror so I could see what was happening.

Was she kidding? I mean, really, I asked her if she was kidding. She said that some women like to see the birthing process. I told her thanks but I really didn't feel the need to see my intestines and other various organs on my stomach. With all of the drugs pumping through my system, the whole procedure was a blur anyway. After twenty-seven hours of labor, through a fog of drugs, I heard a scream and I laughed. Madelyne didn't cry. Oh no. My little girl screamed as if she was nice and comfortable where she was and how *dare* we wake her up.

She was perfect.

She was beautiful. She was born with dark black hair, just like my mother and me. She was the spitting image of Tyler. After the past months of Tyler distancing himself from the pregnancy, he had a look of pure adulation on his face. I wish I had a camera to capture that moment because that was the first and last time I saw genuine emotion toward his daughter.

For me, it was a very surreal moment to hold my child. For someone who never wanted kids and never felt any maternal instinct, those feelings were non-existent when she was placed in my arms.

My beautiful Madelyne Rose.

Chapter 5

Why Don't You Love Her?

It was about two in the morning when our family finally left. The nurses wheeled me to my recovery room. They asked if I wanted Madelyne in the room with us and I said no the same time Tyler said yes. Tyler was mad because he thought I was stepping on his manhood implying that he couldn't take care of Madelyne while I recovered. I didn't care because I had blood clot pads on my legs, a catheter, stitches across my abdomen, and various drugs coursing through my veins. Madelyne was taken to the nursery.

Once Tyler and I were settled into my room, our new nurse came in at 2:30 in the morning with paperwork.

Apparently, it was hospital procedure to go over all information about a newborn baby regardless of the time. I fell asleep during her explanation.

Because I had a C-section, I had to stay in the hospital for three days instead of two. We had a steady stream of visitors: My parents, my aunt, my cousin and his wife, my best friend and her daughter, and my friend Jessica. None of Tyler's family or friends came.

One big bone of contention between Tyler and myself throughout the entire pregnancy was Madelyne's last name. I didn't change my last name when we got married. I really wanted Madelyne to have my last name. My mom even tried to compromise by suggesting that if we had a girl, she would have my last name, and if we had a boy, he would have Tyler's last name. I knew Tyler never got over the fact that I didn't take his name when we got married. When it came time to fill out the birth certificate, even though he didn't show interest in his child, she was going to have his last name. To this day, I regret that decision.

Before we brought Madelyne home, I planned on breastfeeding so I signed up for a session with the lactate nurse. I felt breastfeeding was the best option because of the nutritional values and cost. However, my body wasn't able to produce milk. I was devastated. Tyler wanted me to keep trying. I pumped, tried a couple of different drugs but nothing worked. We had to buy formula. Also, at

Madelyne's first visit to the pediatrician, we were told Madelyne needed special formula with soy. When we found out the cost of a box of formula, Tyler told me I was worthless because not only did I not have a natural birth, but my body couldn't produce milk.

The first two nights Madelyne was home, Tyler and I were still in a fantasy world, until sleep deprivation kicked in. The third night, Tyler came home from work and didn't even hold Madelyne. He ignored us, went upstairs to finish his work, came back down, and went to bed. It was 7:00 in the evening.

I was dumbfounded. What parent of a newborn doesn't want to hold his baby? I fed Madelyne around 9:00 that evening, tucked her in her crib, and went to bed. After getting up with Madelyne twice that night, I was so exhausted I made Tyler get up. He went into her room, shoved a pacifier in her mouth, and went back to bed. He didn't get up with her for the rest of the night. When he left to go to work, he didn't say good-bye.

I began to panic when night came because I knew I wasn't going to get any sleep. I tried to nap when Madelyne napped during the day, but I just wasn't getting an adequate amount of sleep. Also, by the fourth night home from the hospital, I started to feel sick. I had a fever, my stomach hurt, and there was a lot of blood in my urine. I finally called my doctor around 10:00 that night and told her my symptoms. She said to go to the hospital immediately. Tyler was on the bed next to me while I was on the phone so he heard the conversation. As soon as I hung up, he went into a rage.

"You are such a fucking worthless piece of shit!" he screamed at me.

He started throwing books, pillows, anything he could get his hands on. I was in complete disbelief.

"You're pissed because I have to go back to the hospital? Are you serious right now?"

Madelyne started crying in the background. I was standing next to the bed. As he walked past me, he shoved me into the footboard. My stitches started to bleed.

"I'm human," he yelled. "I have a right to be pissed. Just leave me the fuck alone."

I called my parents because I was not about to let him take care of my baby. I also decided not to have him take me to hospital. When my parents came, my dad stayed with Tyler and my mom went to the hospital with me.

As my doctor suspected, I had an infection and I had to be readmitted. As soon as I was settled into my room, I sent my mom back to the house to check on Madelyne.

When Tyler went to work, my parents took Madelyne back to their house. It was decided that when Tyler was done with work, they were all going to visit me at the hospital.

While I was in the hospital I realized something was really wrong about how I felt about Madelyne. I loved her so much that I felt that she deserved a better mother than me. I was just so overwhelmed with everything. I really thought that motherhood shouldn't be so hard and there was something wrong with me. When my doctor came in to see me, I told her what I was feeling.

She said she wasn't surprised that I was showing signs of post-partum depression. She admitted she was concerned throughout my pregnancy because according to the statistics, I was predisposed to post-partum depression because of my anxiety disorder. She asked if it was okay if she sent in a social worker that worked with post-partum patients. I was hesitant but agreed.

When the social worker talked to me about post-partum depression, everything she said made sense. I felt that everyone around me was so excited to have this baby and I was resentful of that excitement. Didn't anyone understand how hard this was? After talking with the social worker for an hour, she said she would come back later to talk with my family when they came to visit me.

When Tyler and my parents came, they brought Madelyne. I was so happy to see her. I knew I loved her. I loved holding her. I loved smelling her. I loved to brush my fingers over her hair. I loved when her little fingers grabbed mine.

I hated myself for not being good enough for this

child. This was what I needed the social worker to tell my family because I didn't know how to express my feelings into words.

As soon as the social worker began explaining the symptoms of post-partum depression, it was obvious my family didn't want to hear what she had to say. The more I felt the tension in the room, I began to think that maybe I didn't have post-partum depression after all. If my family didn't think I had it, then maybe I didn't. After she left, I ripped up her business card and threw it out.

Toward the end of the visit, my parents gave Tyler and me a little privacy. They took Madelyne and waited for him in the lobby.

Tyler stood at the end of my bed. "I'm not mad at you."

"What?" I asked.

"No one is mad that you are here."

Then he left. No hug. No kiss. Not even a handshake. I was shocked. Did he expect me to be thankful or happy that no one was mad at me? What a totally ridiculous asinine thing to say.

After my family left, I tried to sleep but felt completely alone. I knew my parents weren't going to come back up to see me because they took Madelyne for the night. Even though Tyler was able to stay in the room with me overnight, he decided to go home. I called my friend Jessica. I started bawling as I was talking to her.

She wanted to come see me. Jess got in a really bad car accident in high school, so she was apprehensive about driving in certain conditions, especially at night. She knew I needed someone with me and even though it was close to 9:00 at night, she drove to the hospital. She stayed with me for over two hours. She hugged me when I cried. She made me snort with laughter. She even carried my IV bag into the bathroom for me when the antibiotics gave me diarrhea. Now that's a true friend.

While Jess was there, one of the nurses came in and talked to us about how ill-prepared *every* new parent is with a newborn. She gave me the best advice about being a new parent. Never turn away help when it's offered. If someone offers to come over to watch your baby so you can sleep, take it. To this day, that is the *only* advice I give to any of my friends who are impending parents.

After Jess left, I slept for 12 hours straight. My doctor came the next morning and told me I didn't have an infection anymore, but that she would write something down on the chart so I could stay another night. I was so tempted but I felt guilty because I had already spent two nights in the hospital and I felt I needed to take care of my baby.

Tyler picked me up and we went to my parent's house to get Madelyne. I remember sitting on the couch next to Tyler and I had what I can only describe as an out-of-body experience. Tyler was telling my parents about the great amount of sleep he had gotten the past two nights. He made some joke about snoring and everyone laughed. I laughed too but inside I was furious.

Why are you laughing? I thought. *What is so funny? How can you laugh? I have to take this baby home and my life is going to be hell.* My mind was screaming, *Shut the fuck up! Don't you notice how much I hate all of you?*

While I was in the hospital, my parents did talk to Tyler about a plan to help me through the next few months. My mom was going to come over everyday during the week to help with Madelyne so I could get some sleep. Then on the weekends, my parents would take Madelyne back to their house so Tyler and I could spend some time alone. It sounded like a great plan.

By this point, Tyler had flat out stopped helping at night. He didn't even pretend to care when I asked him to get up so I could sleep. So the first morning when my mom came over, I wasn't too upset that I didn't get any sleep the night before because I figured I would be able to sleep during the day. Again, it sounded good except it was hard to sleep when our house was only 1200 square feet and the bedroom was on the same floor as the nursery. At most, I was only getting about two hours of sleep, and it wasn't a very deep sleep either. God bless my mom because not only did she take care of Madelyne while I tried to sleep, she cleaned the house and made dinner for Tyler and me.

After the first two days of "the plan," my mom would make dinner and leave when Tyler came home. By the third night, I was begging my mom to stay because whenever I heard Tyler come home, my anxiety went through the roof. I knew once he was home, my mom would leave and I would be on my own with Madelyne.

My mom noticed something wasn't right, but at the time, was too polite to mention anything. When my mom started staying for dinner, Tyler stopped eating with me. Actually, he stopped everything. All pretend displays of affection for me or for Madelyne were gone. When he walked in the door, he ignored us and went upstairs to the office. When my mom left around seven each night, I started popping Xanax like candy. It was the only way I could get through the night without losing my sanity.

One weekend, Tyler and I decided that we were going to keep Madelyne instead of taking her to my parents, so we could bond as a family. But for me, it was more of a test to see if Tyler would help me on the weekends. Early Saturday morning (really, the middle of the night) Tyler surprised me by getting up when Madelyne cried. There was a catch, though. He asked me to get up with him or else he wasn't going to get up. To me, it didn't make sense that both of us had to get up. We sat in the living room at two in the morning. He was grinning like an idiot as he held Madelyne.

"See? Isn't this perfect?"

I sat on the other couch just staring at him.

"I like this. We're all up together as a family. This is like bonding time."

I smiled at him while thinking, *I don't fucking care about fucking bonding at fucking two in the fucking morning.* (Yes, that many f-bombs were running through my head. Not very motherly, I know.)

Lo and behold, the same thing happened the next night. By the time Sunday morning came, I had a full out panic attack despite the Xanax.

"Tyler. I can't do this. Something needs to change." I was crying hysterically.

He reached over and took Madelyne from me. "Why don't you go upstairs and sleep and I'll take care of Madelyne."

(When we converted our guest room to the nursery, we put the extra bed upstairs in the office.)

Maybe that was all I needed, so I agreed. When I lay down, however, I couldn't sleep because I couldn't trust Tyler with Madelyne. From the day she was born, Tyler had never been alone with her. He couldn't even get up in the middle of the night by himself and take care of her. As I lay on the bed upstairs, I could hear Madelyne cry. I tensed up because I knew Tyler didn't know what to do.

I came back downstairs. "I can't do this. I need to call my mom."

"I knew it. Call your mommy because you can't do

anything yourself."

Before I could stop myself, I yelled, "At least I have a mom who gives a shit about me!"

It was probably one of the meanest things I have ever said in my entire life and I was so sorry I said it but, to be honest, at that moment I just didn't care.

My mom didn't hesitate as she told me to pack a bag for Madelyne and myself. She said we needed to move in there while things got sorted out. I think she was expecting this phone call.

Up to this point, my family and friends had helped me out in every way they could, but my parents turned their lives upside down for us. When Madelyne and I moved in, my parents gave up their master bedroom to me. They slept downstairs and took turns with Madelyne during the night. Both of them insisted that I go to bed by seven every night, especially when my doctor told me that I was not healing properly from the C-section.

She attributed it to the lack of sleep and stress. She talked to me about seeking professional help and gave me a business card of a therapy clinic to see someone who specialized in PPD. Also, it was pretty obvious at this point that Tyler and I were not getting along and that needed to be dealt with as well.

When I first moved into my parent's house, Tyler tried to put a time limit on what he termed, "my visit." He constantly asked me when I was moving back home. He thought I was only going to be there for a week. I kept telling him that I didn't know. What really worried me about moving back home, though, was that Tyler never owned up to the fact that he stopped helping me take care of Madelyne. I learned from some of his friends that he had been telling everyone that he had no idea why I moved out. I was so pissed at him and that was one of the reasons why I couldn't move back home. Until he admitted that he needed to step it up when it came to taking care of Madelyne, I was not about to leave my parent's house. My parents also agreed that they didn't want me to move back home until I was ready.

The main reason why I couldn't move back home was that I was terrified of the nighttime. Even though the situation was different at my parent's house, I instinctively felt panic every night at seven because of what happened when I lived at home. I had to take a sleeping pill at night or else I would panic all night. I kept telling my parents that I would help at night, but they were very adamant that I needed to sleep. They wanted me to heal from the surgery and they told me not to worry about helping until after the holidays.

Speaking of the holidays, Christmas was a disaster. The family agreed to have Christmas at my parent's house because of the baby. My older brother flew home from California (he's 38 and has lived in California since he was 18, but I still call Michigan his home) and saw his niece for first time. It was love at first sight for both of them. My six-foot-six cousin (who is the same age as me) held Madelyne while she slept when we opened gifts. Most of the evening was calm, but toward the later evening, Madelyne started getting fussy.

Tyler and I took her upstairs away from the noise. We were upstairs for 45 minutes, trying to calm her down. We tried everything but nothing worked. Finally I told Tyler I was going to get my mom. I took Madelyne downstairs to ask my mom for help. When we came downstairs and my mom asked what was wrong, Tyler started yelling about how *he* didn't need any help with *his* daughter. He stormed out of the house. He left without his coat, keys, or wallet. He came back after an hour. He sat at the dining room table away from everyone else and didn't say a word.

The plan was for him to stay over at my parent's house that night and we would all have pancakes Christmas morning. When it was time for us to go to bed, Tyler said he was going back home. My mom asked him what was wrong and he said he was leaving because he felt he wasn't needed. He grabbed his stuff and left. No one knew what to say so we all said an awkward goodnight to each other and went our separate ways. The Waltons, we were not.

On Christmas morning, I don't remember who called whom, but Tyler was still pissed that I handed Madelyne over to my mom.

"You're selfish and your family doesn't want me around. They don't want me around Madelyne," he ranted. "I'm sitting at home by myself Christmas morning."

I sighed. "You're doing it to yourself. No one is telling you that you can't come over."

"Do you even want me there? No one even wants me there. I'm just going to sit here by myself all fucking day."

I was so annoyed. It was a whole "feel-sorry-for-Tyler moment" and I was sick of it. "You know what? You're either going to come over or not. You're either going to make it a good Christmas or not. But it's up to you what you want to do because I'm going to make it a good first Christmas for our daughter."

For once, he was actually speechless. It was the first time in a long time I had stood up to him. "Well, I guess I can come over," he sulked. "But only if no one treats me badly."

No one ever did, but whatever.

He came, ate, opened presents, and left early. I think he stayed maybe two hours. He called me that night.

"I hate being a parent," he blurted out. "When my friends ask me how it is to be a parent, I tell them not to do it."

Wow, I thought. *That's the father of my child.* He was telling people not to have children. It was devastating to hear that. I hung up on him.

He only called me once between Christmas and New Year's Eve but never stopped by to see Madelyne. He told me he was going to come over and spend the night so he could be with us for the New Year. Since we were supposed to do that for Christmas, you can imagine how that turned out.

When he arrived, he pulled me aside and said he wanted to take Madelyne home for New Year's Day. There was a catch. He didn't want me to come with him. Oh *hell* no.

"Are you serious?" I stared at him.

"I just feel like I'm not allowed to be a parent when I'm here."

"You just told me a week ago you hated being a parent."

That pissed him off. Now he was on the defense. "I want to try to see if I can be a good parent with her by myself."

I exploded. "She's not a fucking experiment, Tyler! She's a baby! You don't know how to take care of her because you're never here!" By this time, my parents came into the room.

"What's going on?" my mom asked.

I started crying. "Tyler wants to take Madelyne back home tomorrow by himself."

"Why do you always have to involve your parents in

everything?" screamed Tyler.

My mom tried to calm Tyler down. "Tyler, Madelyne is really a handful. She's been acting colicky lately. It takes all three of us to take care of her. Why put that burden on yourself when you don't have to?"

"You just want my baby all to yourselves!" Tyler was out of control. "This is what you wanted! Now that she's here, you don't want me around."

My dad tried to intervene. "Tyler, that's not true. Our door is always open to you. You're always welcome here."

"I don't fucking need this. I don't need any of you." He stormed out—again. He never wished us a Happy New Year.

છળ્છ

I didn't hear from Tyler until late evening on New Year's Day and he was revved.

"I know there is a conspiracy between you and your parents to keep Madelyne away from me."

I rolled my eyes. "Tyler, have we ever locked you out of the house? Have I ever told you not to come over? Where are you getting this from?"

"My f—friends are telling me that you are n—never coming home," he sputtered. "They tell me that you just wanted my sperm and now you want to get rid of me."

I was dealing with a lunatic. Did he honestly think that his genetic material was ideal? He was handsome, I'll give him that. But as far as intelligence? Not so much.

I tried to alleviate his fear. "Tyler, I am coming home. I'm here because I need my parents' help because neither one of us has any experience with a newborn."

"But how am I going to get any experience if I never get the chance to be with her?"

I sighed. "Again, you have to put the effort in. No one has told you that you can't come over here. You need to start coming over here more."

"Why can't you just move home?" he whined.

"Because I have to get used to taking care of Madelyne on my own. I still get nervous when I am alone with her all day."

"Well, I guess we're fucked," he snapped.

I was stunned. "*What did you just say?*"

He knew he just screwed up big time. "No, Megan. It was something the cats just did. I was yelling at them."

"Really? You're going to blame your stupidity on the cats?"

"No!" he roared. "The cats did something!"

I hung up on him.

The next day, Tyler called and acted as though nothing had happened. He asked when Madelyne and I were planning on moving back home. I told him, for the hundredth time, I needed my parents' help during the day and at night to take care of Madelyne. He told me that taking care of a baby wasn't that difficult and that it was time I learned how. He told me I had until the end of the month or he was going to bring Madelyne home. This time, he hung up on me. I knew I had to see a therapist. My marriage was crumbling fast and I needed help with the pieces.

The day before my first session with the therapist, I got into my car and there was a CD from Tyler. The note from Tyler said, "I love you and we will work this out." I popped in the CD and it was some dumb love song I had never heard before. Halfway through the song, I pulled the out the CD and broke it in half. Tyler knew damn well I was going to therapy more about our marriage than post-partum depression and he was trying to brainwash me into thinking that everything was hunky-dory. I was so disgusted.

In the beginning stages of therapy, my therapist suggested that I go back home every weekend, by myself, to spend time with Tyler to work on our marriage. The first night I went to stay, we sat in bed and talked.

"What do you feel right now? Don't even think—just say," I asked him.

"I hate being a parent." Bam. First thing that came out of his mouth. But he wasn't finished. "I miss our old life. If we had the choice to do it all over again, I would never have had the baby. I don't even care about her."

Then he hugged me. "Can we have sex?"

He was so disgusting to me. I didn't want him to touch me. I didn't want to touch him. I didn't want to sleep in the same bed as him. I didn't want to be in the same house as him. There was a snowstorm that night, but I told him I really needed to go back to my parents' house. After that weekend, Tyler only came to see Madelyne every Thursday for an hour and every Sunday for five hours. During this time he spent four of those hours watching the football game with my dad while my dad took care of Madelyne.

When my therapist asked how Tyler and I were coping on the weekends, I told her I only went back to the house to get some more of my things and to see my cats. I missed my cats more than Tyler.

My therapist suggested I bring Tyler to our next session. Surprisingly, he agreed. For most of the session, my therapist tried to figure out if our marriage was worth saving. At the end of the session, she asked both of us to think of one quality that each of us had that made the other one happy.

I looked at Tyler. "I love how you know when I'm feeling anxious about something and you reach over and grab my hand and give me a squeeze and I know everything is going to be all right."

Tyler looked at my therapist. "I like her cooking."

When he said that, I was devastated. It was like a

punch to the gut. The next day, I went to our house to grab some more of my things and called my doctor in tears.

"Please," I sobbed. "I need some more meds. Just something. You need to help me. "

"Megan," she said calmly. "I can't help you any-more. You need to go to the hospital. They will help you."

Tyler was at work, so I called my parents so some-one could drive me to the hospital. My dad and aunt came to the house. I called Tyler to let him know what was go-ing on.

He said he was working and told me to call him if something happened.

When we got to the hospital, the ER doctor gave me Ativan right away because I could barely breathe. I still didn't understand how they were going to treat me. The social worker on call came to see me and asked me a bunch of questions.

When she told me I didn't need to be committed, but that she strongly suggested that I voluntarily admit my-self to the psychiatric ward, I was shocked.

The psych ward? I'm not crazy. I kept trying to tell her to give me medication so I could leave.

She pulled up a chair next to my bed and laid her hand on top of mine.

"Megan, you are not going to get better if you leave

here today as you are. The only way you can take care of your baby is if you voluntarily admit yourself to the hospital." She looked at me. "You are not crazy. You need help. Please let us help you."

I glanced at my dad and aunt. They were both crying.

I nodded. "Okay."

Chapter 6

Am I Crazy?

On February 4, 2011, I was admitted to the psychiatric ward for the first time. My dad and I had said good-bye in the ER. He was going to visit later during visiting hours and bring a duffel bag of clothes.

When an orderly dropped me off in the ward, an intake nurse was waiting for me. She already had the form from the social worker I spoke with in the ER. She took me into a back room and asked me what was wrong.

I broke down. "Am I crazy? Why am I in the psych ward? I've never been somewhere like this. How did this happen?

As with everyone else I had encountered that day, she was extremely nice. "Something is wrong and you need help. We're going to figure out what's going on."

When we got to the end of the intake process she said I could change from my hospital gown into the comfy clothes I wore to the hospital. I let out a *huge* sigh of relief. Okay, so this wasn't like *One Flew Over the Cuckoo's Nest*.

The nurse led me to my room. There weren't any locks on the doors, but she did have to take my shoelaces. At least each room had its own bathroom. There was a young woman in the other bed. I didn't look at her because I was too embarrassed. The nurse told me that because it was late in the afternoon, there wasn't anything on the schedule except dinner and visiting hours. Since my dad hadn't brought my bag of clothes and books, I didn't have much to do so I lay down on the bed. It wasn't long before the nurses called us to dinner.

The dining area was like a cafeteria with two long tables and one small table for the patients with eating disorders. I found my tray and sat down. I didn't try to talk to anyone. I just listened instead. Everyone seemed normal, but I'm not sure what I was expecting. No one was throwing food, yelling, hitting himself or others, or anything else I had seen in movies. I ate what was edible on my tray (which wasn't much) and went back to my room.

Not long after, my roommate came back. I don't remember her name, so I will call her Erin. She was young, either 23 or 24. She was in the ward for anxiety disorder. I was shocked. I didn't know people could go to a mental health ward for anxiety disorder. When I was first diagnosed at 19, I had a really hard time dealing with the constant anxiety, so I really commended her for seeking help. She was married and her husband was completely supportive. In fact, he was visiting her that night so they could talk about her transfer to an outpatient program the next day.

When the visiting hour arrived, my dad and Tyler came to see me. That was the first time I had seen or spoken to Tyler that day because he hadn't come to the hospital with me. It was awkward because he acted like he didn't know what to say. He stood at the foot of my bed and just stared at me. He didn't even say anything. My dad and I talked about Madelyne most of the time. We tried to include Tyler in the conversation, but after a while, we just talked between the two of us. The ward gave us the option of bringing the kids to visit their parents, but I didn't want Madelyne at the hospital. It sounded silly because she was obviously too young to understand what was going on, but I didn't want her to see me in the mental health ward. I had her pictures and kept them on my nightstand.

With about ten minutes left in the visiting hour, my dad gave Tyler and me some privacy and left the room. I tried to talk to him about what had happened that day, but all he wanted to talk about was his rights as a father. I remember how vile I thought he was at that moment.

I knew exactly what he was doing. He knew how much I distrusted him with Madelyne. I also knew how much he didn't even care about her. But here he was, telling me that he had rights as a father and that while I was in the hospital, my parents didn't have any legal standing to keep Madelyne at their house. I didn't say a goddamn word. I knew damn well he didn't have the balls to take Madelyne home and take care of her. And sure enough, I was right. Not once, during the entire five days I was in the hospital, did he ask my parents to let him take care of Madelyne, nor did he visit or call them to see how she was. I was relieved when he left.

After visiting hours, Erin talked me into going to the common area and playing games with the other patients. She explained to me that in this type of environment, the therapists and nurses wanted to see the patients out of their rooms and interacting. In the short time that I knew Erin, I was glad she was my first roommate. She made me laugh and feel positive about being in what could be deemed a depressing place. When she left the next day, we exchanged e-mail addresses, but I never heard from her again. I hope she is doing well, wherever she is.

The next day, I finally met my new doctor for the first time. Dr. Post was an elderly gentleman. I usually don't like male doctors. The only male doctor I ever had was my pediatrician until I hit puberty. In the psych ward, the doctors were assigned to the patients so I didn't have a choice. I didn't care. I just wanted to know what was wrong.

When we met, he asked me what I thought was wrong. I blurted out what was going on. I had never felt like this. I told him that I didn't even know why I was in the psych ward. I was crying and blubbering. He listened to everything and summed it up perfectly:

"Megan, you just had a baby, you have anxiety disorder, post-partum depression, your marriage is in trouble, and you are in law school. I'm surprised it took you this long to feel this way."

In that one statement, he made me feel so much better about being where I was. He wasn't judging me. I wasn't another crazy person he had to deal with. I was here because I had a problem, and he was here to fix it.

After we talked, Dr. Post prescribed medications. I was already on Lexapro for my anxiety and Vicodin for my C-section. He added Cymbalta and Seroquel for the post-partum depression, Ativan for the panic attacks, and Ambien for sleep. Before Dr. Post left, he went over the HIPPA form with me. Usually a spouse is the person listed, but I specifically told Dr. Post that I wanted to list my parents instead. Something told me not to put down Tyler's name. I didn't want Dr. Post to share any information with him. That decision ended up being a blessing in disguise, which became more apparent in the future. This ended up being one of the best decisions I made during that time.

I was admitted to the hospital right before the weekend, so I spent a couple of days in the ward before I had my first group therapy session. In my first session, a lot of people had questions for me. I had decided that nothing was off limits. I was going to be open and honest with everyone. After the first fifteen minutes, ten strangers who I had never met before and would never see again, made me realize that emotional abuse is a form of domestic violence and that it was not okay. These people told me I deserved better. I knew my marriage was over. Tyler probably did too because he never came back to visit me.

I was in the hospital for five days. On the last day, Dr. Post made sure I had a doctor on the outside to write meds and a therapist to see on a weekly basis. In addition, he suggested I call my law school advisor to explain what was going on and ask if I could take off the current semester and readmit the next semester. Dr. Post also suggested I talk to my therapist about my marriage. He never said to file for divorce. No one ever talked me into filing for divorce. It was my decision, and my decision alone. By that time, I was comfortable enough with Dr. Post to say I was going to file for divorce.

I left the hospital and went back to my parents'

house. The new drug regimen made me tired, but I definitely felt better about myself. I knew these were the steps I needed to take to make myself feel better.

I called my advisor at school. She was very understanding. She knew I was going to come back. She just wanted me to get better. She said I would always have a place at school. Next, I called the clinic and scheduled an appointment with the clinic doctor and my new therapist.

After I made my phone calls, I told my parents that I was going to file for divorce. My parents were surprised because they thought while I was in the hospital, I was going to learn techniques about how to work on my marriage. That's when I finally opened up to them about the life I had been living with Tyler during our marriage. I didn't tell them everything, just enough to let them know why I wanted to file for divorce. I told them my self-esteem was low. I felt like I had absolutely no self-worth. The constant emotional abuse had knocked me down to nothing. My dad knew of a family law attorney. We were able to see him right away.

Cue Don McGinnis. He is, hands down, the best attorney I have *ever* had the privilege of meeting, working with, and watching in action. He is very straight-forward and will give you the answer that you might not want to hear, but that you need to hear. When my dad and I sat in his office that day, I didn't get into too much detail. Don asked if Tyler knew that I was planning to file for divorce and I told him I didn't know. As of that moment, it was a race to the courthouse. In filing for divorce, it's always better to file as the Plaintiff. The Plaintiff has the advantage of the jurisdiction (county) to file in and the advantage of testifying first if we were going to go to trial. Don told us that we would meet later to discuss the details of the divorce but not to tell Tyler that I was filing for divorce. Don also told us to start keeping a log of everything Tyler did whether positive or negative.

It was a Thursday when we met. We wouldn't be able to file the divorce papers until Monday and we didn't want Tyler to run out and file before us. Tyler came over that night but I didn't see him. I had my parents tell him that I was tired because I didn't know what to say. I didn't call him that Friday or Saturday.

That Sunday he came over. He sat in the rocking chair, holding Madelyne. I sat on the couch. I tried to not talk to him. He talked about how great it would be when I moved back home. He just kept going on and on. I couldn't take it anymore. I knew he couldn't go to the courthouse that day to file because it was Sunday and he was not going to be able to find an attorney the next morning in time to file before us.

I had to tell him. "Tyler, I filed for divorce."

He rocked back and forth a few times. Then he finally looked at me and said, "How long do I have until I have to move out?"

Chapter 7

Meet My Real Ex-Husband

Tyler handed Madelyne back to me and left. My parents asked me what had happened. I wasn't crying. I felt relieved. Six hours later, he called my parents landline because I wasn't answering my cell phone. He asked me why I was doing this to him. My parents told me to hang up. I told him I couldn't talk to him about it and not to contact me until he settled down and then we could figure things out. From February eleventh to nineteenth, Tyler never called about Madelyne nor came over to see her.

The divorce papers were filed on Monday. For those who are not familiar with divorce papers, the plaintiff

files what is called a Complaint For Divorce. It lists facts
such as the plaintiff's residence, the date of marriage, the
parties' date of separation, any children involved in the
marriage, and anything else pertinent.

The next set of papers filed in court are from the defendant. They are called the Answer to Complaint For
Divorce. It either agrees or disagrees with what is listed
in the Complaint. Usually the Complaint and the Answer
are in agreement. However, Tyler was very unpredictable
and his Answer to Complaint wasn't any different. In his
Answer, he agreed that we were married and the date we
were married. In answer to the standard listing of "Plaintiff is not at this time pregnant," defendant neither admitted nor denied the allegation, meaning he didn't know if I
was pregnant. He knew that we hadn't had sex in over a
year, so this was his way of stating on a court record that
I might be sleeping around. Unlike Tyler who had found
a new girlfriend two weeks after I filed for divorce, sex
was *the* last thing on my mind. The defendant also denied
the allegation that the plaintiff (me) was suited to care,
have custody and control of Madelyne. This was even
though the *defendant* had never been alone with Madelyne in the three months that she had been alive.

The most telling Answer to the Complaint was that
Tyler adamantly insisted that the court should not order a
Temporary Restraining Order Against Property Transfer.
In plain English, this meant that Tyler would be allowed

to take money out of our bank account. While the attorneys were working on the legal paperwork, Tyler and I talked about how long he could stay in the house. My parents and I agreed that he could stay until he found someplace else to live as long as the stay wasn't excessive.

Most importantly, however, I wanted him to know that he could still come over anytime to see Madelyne. I never once kept him away from her. No matter how I felt about Tyler, he was Madelyne's father and he needed to bond with her.

Tyler kept trying to call me to work things out. I never answered my phone. When he came over to see Madelyne, it was obvious that he was using these visitations to see me, not Madelyne. I finally confronted him and told him I had made my decision. It was time for him to move on.

Meanwhile, Don was suspicious of the answers given in the Answers to the Complaint. Don filed an immediate Temporary Restraining Order Against Property Transfer, which was signed immediately by our Family Court Judge. The order stated the plaintiff (myself) would suffer unwarranted loss of property rights unless the misconduct was restrained. In other words, Tyler was not allowed to remove anything from the house nor from our bank account without talking to me first.

Sure enough, Don was right. When I went back to

the house for the first time since filing for divorce, Tyler had made sure to remove the items he wanted: our brand new flat screen TV, Keruig coffee maker, all of his guitars and equipment, and the PS3. I also saw my favorite black cocktail dress hanging on the bathroom door. (I later found out that Tyler's new girlfriend liked to play dress-up with my clothes.)

My next stop was the bank. The bank teller told me that there had been a recent withdrawal of $4,590 from our joint savings account and $650 from our joint checking account leaving me with a total of $87 to buy diapers and formula. Don wrote a letter to Tyler's attorney requesting the return of the money, but to no avail. I knew I was never going to see that money again.

On Sunday, February twentieth, I finally called Tyler to ask if he was going to stop by to see Madelyne. I called him around 10:00 and he finally responded around 11:00. He said that he was going to be in the area around 5:00 and wanted to take Madelyne to a friend's house. I told him that I wasn't comfortable with him taking her out of the house because he hadn't seen her in almost two weeks.

He responded, "I don't think it's a good day for me to stop over. Have a good weekend." He never asked about Madelyne. Tyler didn't see Madelyne between February twenty-first and March second.

My next meeting with Don was regarding temporary

custody of Madelyne. Don agreed that I should keep temporary custody of Madelyne. He filed a motion for a Temporary Custody Hearing for March 2, 2011. We stated that I was best suited for the temporary and permanent care, custody and control of the minor child. Before the hearing, Don and I suggested a parenting time agreement:

- Tyler has parenting time every:
  - Thursday from 6:30-7:30
  - Sunday from 12:00-5:00
  - Tyler shall not remove Madelyne from my home during his parenting time
- Parenting time will be reviewed on or after April 1, 2010

Tyler never argued the motion.

He had also stopped paying the utility, water, and cable bills at our house. I began to receive phone calls from bill collectors because all the bills were in my name. I called Don to ask him what to do and he asked why we had we allowed Tyler to stay at the house. He said to file an eviction notice right away. The eviction notice allowed Tyler thirty days to move from the house before we could begin court proceedings. To make Tyler feel *really* uncomfortable in the house, Don suggested we remove the cable since it was in my name and the house was in my parents' name.

My dad and I turned our cable removal mission into a James Bond Covert Mission. It was hilarious. We didn't say a word as we drove to the house. My dad parked at the end of the driveway, in case Tyler came home from work. We didn't want him to block us in. We walked into the house, knowing our respective missions. Dad unplugged the TV cable box and I raced upstairs to unplug the Ethernet cable box. We were in and out in five minutes. It was a stealth operation.

I thought for sure I was going to get a scathing phone call that night, but I didn't hear a word. When I went to the house a few days later, I noticed a note on the table. It was a "to-do" list for Tyler's attorney. At the top of the list was: *Took cable! Can we sue??!!*

I busted out laughing. Obviously, Tyler began to see me as the enemy. Don told me that in order to avoid any confrontations, I should either not be at the house or stay upstairs during Tyler's visits with Madelyne.

On March third, I texted Tyler to find out if he was coming over on his scheduled visitation day. (He hadn't seen Madelyne since February eleventh.) He stopped by at 6:30. He changed three clean diapers and fed her one-ounce of formula. She cried almost the entire time. Tyler held her but talked to my dad instead of playing with Madelyne. As soon as he left, my dad held Madelyne and she stopped crying almost instantly.

On Sunday, March sixth, Tyler's allotted time was

from 12-5. He texted me the day before to let me know he was only coming over between 12-2. I asked him why he didn't stay the whole time and he stated he had more important things to do. I asked him what in God's name was more important than spending time with his daughter. He hung up.

Per Don's instructions, (and unbeknownst to Tyler) we kept a log of Tyler's visits:

- Sunday, March 13: Tyler couldn't come over because he was moving out of the house.
- Thursday, March 17: Tyler arrived at 6:30. He left 15 minutes early when he couldn't get Madelyne to stop crying.
- Sunday, March 20: Tyler stayed two hours instead of his four hour visit because he couldn't get Madelyne to stop crying. He became aggressive with Madelyne and I told him to leave.

I called Tyler that night because I knew he was getting frustrated when Madelyne cried and I was afraid he was going to hurt her. He was evasive on the phone and wouldn't answer any questions. I told him I was going to call my attorney to ask him for advice. Don suggested that I have someone sit in the room with Tyler in case there was an incident. I called Tyler and informed him that my dad was going to sit in the room with him. He said that was fine and hung up.

On Thursday, March thirty-first, Tyler showed up at 6:30. This was the first supervised visit. My dad had set-up his computer in the living room to do some work. After Tyler arrived and played with Madelyne for a few minutes, he wanted to know why my dad was in the room. Tyler claimed that he didn't know the visits were now supervised. (Apparently he forgot about our phone call only four days previous.) Tyler spent the next forty minutes defending his character to my dad and asking how my dad felt about him. My dad was non-responsive and said he didn't want to get involved.

Tyler started becoming aggressive so my dad offered advice on how to play with Madelyne. Tyler said he had enough and began to leave. He tried again to defend himself in the hallway. Before he left, Tyler asked my dad if he would try to stop him if he took Madelyne out of the house. My dad was stunned by the question. He said he wouldn't use physical restraint. My mom overheard the question and said she would call the police. Tyler left.

On April fifth, Don received a Motion Regarding Parenting Time from Tyler's attorney. A hearing was scheduled for May 4, 2011. Tyler's attorney argued the following: Tyler had consistently exercised his parenting time as currently ordered, Tyler should be entitled to expand parenting time, and that he be allowed to take the minor child out of my home during his parenting time. (In Tyler's attorney's defense, he was completely snowed by his client. He had absolutely no idea that Tyler had not followed his parenting time. He was (and is) a wonderful attorney and just had the misfortune to have a very good liar as a client.) Two days after his attorney filed the motion, Tyler screwed himself.

On Thursday, April seventh, he arrived at 6:30 for his visit. My dad was in the living room with his computer. After Tyler arrived and played with Madelyne for a few minutes, he once again wanted to know why my dad was in the living room. Tyler stated that his lawyer had not told him that the visits were now supervised. He then spent most of the next ten minutes waving legal papers in front of my dad, asking him to show Tyler where it said the visits were supervised.

My dad said it was a custody matter and that I had temporary custody and could dictate visitation conditions. All this time, Madelyne was crying.

I was leaving the house for an appointment but I stopped and asked Tyler to leave since he was obviously not there to take care of Madelyne. I told him if he didn't leave, I would call the police.

"Do it," Tyler taunted me. "Call the police."

"Fine." I dialed 911.

Meanwhile, Tyler continued to taunt my dad. "Do

you let your daughter run your house? Does she tell you what to do? Does she hold you by the balls?"

"911 Operator."

"Yes, I need police over to my house," I cried into the phone.

"What is the matter, ma'am?"

"My ex-husband won't leave and he's becoming very aggressive. I'm scared of him. I have a baby and I scared for my baby."

Tyler made fun of me in the background. "Yeah, she's really scared. Keep crying. Keep acting for them, bitch. You stupid bitch." He turned to my dad. "Did you raise her to be this stupid? God, you must have felt sorry for her growing up."

"Do you know if he has any weapons?" the operator asked.

I was still crying. "I know that his dad has guns. I don't know if he has any. He has an anger problem."

Tyler started laughing. "Oh, now I carry guns. If I did, I would have shot her stupid ass a long time ago."

"We will have officers to your house right away," said the operator.

"Thank you." I hung up.

I told my mom to take Madelyne upstairs, walked to the front door, opened it, and waited for the police. Tyler followed me.

He stood next to me.

"Get away from me," I muttered to him.

He smiled. "Really? Make me."

"Who does this, Tyler? Who stays in someone's house when they are asked to leave?"

"I do." He snickered. "Because then I get to see you arrested."

"You're disgusting." I looked right into his eyes. "Move the fuck away from me."

"Or what?" he asked. "What are you going to do? You don't sound too stable right now. Do you think you might need to go back to the psych ward again? You think you're going crazy again?"

I walked back into the kitchen. Tyler followed me. The police arrived soon after. Two officers asked Tyler to step outside and two officers came inside to talk to my dad and me.

Tyler showed the officers what he claimed were legal papers and asked them to show him where it was stated that visits were supposed to be supervised.

The police explained to Tyler that it was not their job to review legal papers and make child custody decisions.

Meanwhile, the officers inside the house asked my dad and me why the visits were supervised. I explained the conversations between my attorney and myself.

The officers repeated to us what they told Tyler. Legal decisions were up to the courts, not the police officers. The officers then told us that Tyler seemed agitated

and that he and his partner were going to escort Tyler off
the property. They waited until Tyler had driven off.

The next day, I called Don to inform him of what
had happened the previous night. He sent a fax to Tyler's
attorney:

> *Dear xxxx:*
>
> *Unfortunately last night during your cli-
> ent's parenting time, Megan and her father
> were forced to call the Troy police. Your cli-
> ent became angry and aggressive during his
> visit.*
>
> *My client is attempting to get a copy of
> the police reports, which won't be ready until
> Monday.*
>
> *A copy will be forwarded to you accord-
> ingly.*
>
> *In the meantime, my client is apprehen-
> sive and afraid to allow Tyler back into her
> home.*
>
> *To that end, she will NOT be allowing
> parenting time on Sunday, April 10th.*
>
> *I realize that you have filed a motion,
> which is currently scheduled for May 4, 2011,
> to expand his parenting time. Hopefully, we
> can work out a resolution to this current is-
> sue prior to that date.*

Needless to say, the motion for parenting time was cancelled because Tyler never fought temporary custody.

On April twelfth, Tyler and I had to go to our first Friend of the Court meeting. We met with our court assigned referee and then had to watch a video about divorce and children. Tyler never said a word to me.

After we left, I got into my car. I was surprised when Tyler knocked on my window. He talked to me for five minutes about the video. It was a random conversation. I started to tell him about Madelyne because I had just taken her to the doctor's for an ear infection. Tyler walked away.

That Thursday, Tyler came over for his first visit since the police incident. My dad decided not to sit in the living room with him to avoid any more confrontations. He let Tyler know about Madelyne's ear infection. It was in her right ear, so he told Tyler to be careful with that ear. Tyler asked what medication she had been prescribed. When my dad told Tyler it was penicillin, Tyler asked how many times a day and how much was dropped in her ear. Seriously.

My dad explained that penicillin doesn't go into the ear but is given orally. Then my dad handed Madelyne over to Tyler.

Madelyne immediately began to cry. My dad left the room and told Tyler that he would be in the next room if he needed anything. Madelyne continued to cry and be-

came louder. After a few minutes, my dad suggested Tyler give Madelyne some formula. My dad prepared the
bottle and gave it to Tyler. Madelyne drank all the formula and still continued to cry. Tyler gave her some more
formula (without telling my Dad) to try to calm her
down.

She drank it and instantly spit it up because her
tummy was full. She cried even louder. After a while,
Madelyne finally cried herself to sleep. When she woke
up about twenty minutes later, Tyler quickly handed her
over to my dad and left. Madelyne quit crying as soon as
he left. We gave her a bath and she was smiling and
laughing. She went to bed without crying.

Before the next visit, we made sure Madelyne had a
long nap and was fed so hopefully she wouldn't cry the
entire time she was with Tyler. Our plan worked. When
Tyler arrived, Madelyne didn't cry for the first fifty
minutes.

Right after I filed for divorce, I began to go back to
church. I was raised Catholic and found comfort in my
faith. Most Sundays, I timed my mass to coincide with
Tyler's visit.

I would arrive home and go immediately upstairs.
This particular Sunday, however, Tyler asked to talk to
me. When I walked into the living room, he was holding
Madelyne, rocking her gently back and forth.

"Hi," I said. "How is she?"

"I don't want joint custody," he blurted out. "You can have her."

Absolutely repulsed by him, I walked away without another word. Tyler handed Madelyne to my dad and left.

Before his next visit, I texted Tyler to let him know neither that myself nor my dad were going to be present, however, my mom was going to be at home to help him if he needed her. Tyler had long blamed my mom for the divorce. He called and told me that he would not be coming over. Before he hung up, though, he told me to check the porch that evening because he was going to drop something off for Madelyne.

When I checked the porch later that night, sure enough, Tyler left something wrapped in a grocery bag. When I opened it up, there was a card, two plastic flowers and a box of chocolates. The card was for me. The two plastic flowers were Madelyne's Easter present. The box of chocolates was my Easter present, which had significant meaning between Tyler and myself. It was an inside joke to give each other a box of chocolates as a gift for every holiday.

I was disgusted. First, two plastic flowers was his Easter gift for his daughter? Second, the box of chocolates cost more than the flowers and I didn't even want them.

Third, dropping off these gifts meant he wasn't coming over to see Madelyne during the Easter weekend even though I knew he had Friday, Saturday, and Sunday off from work.

I threw the chocolates away. He never called to wish Madelyne a Happy Easter and we didn't hear or see him again for a week.

The next time Tyler came over, he arrived at noon. My dad greeted him at the front door. By this time, Tyler walked into our house liked he owned the place. Such arrogance. My dad let Tyler know that Madelyne was still sleeping and told him that she would probably wake up in about 15 minutes.

Before my dad could suggest that he wait, Tyler left. My dad called him ten minutes later when Madelyne woke up and left a message on his voicemail. Tyler didn't come back again until 1:00. My dad fixed a bottle and handed it to Tyler. He fed Madelyne, burped her, and she fell back asleep. Tyler left at 2:00.

Meanwhile, my attorney and I had concerns about Tyler's parenting ability. Don wrote the following letter to Tyler's attorney:

> Dear Mr. xxxx,
>
> Before we would entertain any change in the parenting time schedule, we would suggest that Tyler involve himself in a parenting class.
>
> For your benefit, I am enclosing a list of

programs in Oakland County, which would really benefit Tyler.

One of the problems that seems to exist during his parenting time is that Tyler is frustrated with the child crying, diaper changes and other issues which are basic parenting skills.

Please see to it that he has an opportunity to attend one of these classes.

Tyler's attorney's response:

Dear Mr. McGinnis,

This will acknowledge receipt of your correspondence dated April 19, 2011. I have forwarded same to my client and he suggested that he enroll in one of the courses of his choice.

However, we do believe that it would benefit everyone if your client also attended one of these courses.

Thank you in advance for your anticipated cooperation.

To say that I was angry when I received a copy of that letter would be a huge understatement. I had been taking care of this baby since the day she was born, but

Tyler thought I needed parenting classes? Don said it was just a legal tactic but I knew better. Tyler did it to get a rise out of me. And boy did he ever? But I never gave him the satisfaction of letting him know it.

The next day, Madelyne had a doctor's appointment. After I checked her in, I sat down in the waiting room. The nurse called me to the reception desk to speak to me privately.

"Ms. Cyrulewski, do you know you have an outstanding balance?" she asked.

"No," I answered, confused. "My ex-husband's insurance is supposed to cover Madelyne's doctor's appointments."

"There is a $20 co-pay for each appointment," she explained. "We have tried calling your ex-husband numerous times and have sent two letters to his residence but we haven't heard back from him."

Typical. Whenever money was involved, Tyler ran in the opposite direction. I sighed. "How much does he owe?"

The nurse looked at the chart. "Two-hundred dollars."

I apologized. "I will call him as soon as I get home today."

"Well, actually, we need a payment today because this is an overdue balance."

In other words, the doctor wouldn't see Madelyne

because of the outstanding bill. The poor nurse couldn't even look at me because she was so embarrassed.

"I understand." I pulled out my credit card. "I'll just pay the co-pays after each appointment from now on."

The nurse smiled. "Thank you. I'll make a note on the chart."

☙❦❧

Throughout the summer of 2011, Tyler's visits were sporadic. He liked to play games to see what he could get away with. For example, in the agreement with the Friend of the Court, Tyler had to give me 48 hours notice if he was going to bring any visitors to the house. Also, he wasn't allowed to take Madelyne out of the house except for a walk in the stroller. Tyler had never taken her out before. So one Sunday in June, when I was at church, Tyler decided to take her for a walk in the stroller. It was eighty-eight degrees outside. I never take her for a walk when it's that hot. My dad tried to tell Tyler that it was too hot, but he wouldn't listen. He took her out of the house and didn't even take any water for her. (But he remembered to take water for himself.) He was gone for an hour. When he came back, Madelyne was red, flushed, and screaming. Tyler said a quick good-bye and left.

I quickly undressed her and applied cool clothes all over her body while my dad gave her a bottle of water. I knew exactly why Tyler was gone for so long. One of his best friends had just recently moved into the adjoining subdivision and I knew it was only a matter of time before Tyler tried to take Madelyne over there. Sure enough, the first time Tyler was allowed to take her out of the house, he did what he felt like doing, because he felt that rules didn't apply to him. I called Tyler later that evening and asked him straight out if that's what happened. He admitted that he did take Madelyne to his friend's house. He acted like it wasn't a big deal. I told him he wasn't allowed to take Madelyne outside of the house anymore.

During the month of July, Tyler's emotional disconnection toward Madelyne was becoming more apparent each visit. He never asked for an update on her eating or playing habits. I let him know about her immunization shots in advance and instead of offering to come to the pediatrician's office, he cancelled his visit.

For three weeks in a row he either showed up late or left early. He tried to take Madelyne out for a walk again but the temperature was 90 degrees with a heat index of 95. Only an idiot would take a baby out in that heat. I told him I would call the police if he tried to take her outside. He left early that day.

When he did stay for his visits, he couldn't calm Madelyne down if she was fussy. If she cried, he didn't know if she was hungry or needed her diaper changed. If my dad offered to help him, he refused even if it meant Madelyne cried the entire time.

Toward the end of July, I was back in the mental health ward for another five days. I couldn't take the stress. The divorce date was looming and we still hadn't reached an agreement. Tyler now insisted he wanted joint custody. He *knew* that was my worst fear and he was doing everything in his power to get back at me. He didn't want Madelyne. That was evident even when I was pregnant. He had one goal, and one goal only, make my life a living hell. If threatening joint custody was the way to do that, then by God, he was going to find a way to make that happen.

I also felt incredibly guilty about living with my parents. Not only had they opened their home for Madelyne and me, they opened their bank account as well. Luckily for me, my parents are very financially stable so they kept telling me not to worry about money, but how could I not? I was 33, with a baby, living with my parents and back in school without an income. Not only were my parents supporting me, they were supporting my child because Tyler had not contributed anything financially toward Madelyne.

Also, I didn't know when I was going to graduate from law school. I had dropped the previous semester, just dropped a course from the present semester, and didn't know what I was going to do for the next semester, considering I was back in the hospital again. I knew it was going to be at *least* another two years before I would graduate.

Tyler knew I felt ashamed about having to live off of my parents so every chance he got, he would take digs at me. "Did Mommy make your bed this morning?" or "Did Daddy pay your bills?"

I felt guilty every morning from when I woke until I went to bed at night. I then felt that way all over again the next day.

Tyler had also threatened on numerous occasions that because of my "mental health issues," he felt that Madelyne would be better off in foster care than with me. There were some nights, despite taking a sleeping pill, when I would panic every time I heard a siren. I would wake my mom up just so she could sit with me because I was so scared. Don reassured me dozens of times that the police were not going to come and take Madelyne, but I still felt that, somehow, Tyler would be able to manipulate the system. Whenever I received a text from Tyler threatening foster care, those nights were horrendous. I couldn't even use sleep as an escape. I would lay awake all night and wonder when the police were coming.

I called this stay in the hospital a "tune-up." My doctor adjusted my medications and I talked about my concerns in group therapy. By the time I left, I definitely felt better but only because of the medication adjustments. I knew it would take a lot of work in my weekly therapy sessions to overcome my fear of Tyler, his threats of custody, and my guilt of living with and being supported by my parents.

When I got home, my parents updated me on Tyler's log of visitations. We hadn't told Tyler I was back in the hospital. My parents made up excuses for my absence. The visits were typical Tyler. Either he arrived late or he left early. My dad had to fix the bottle or calm Madelyne down himself when Tyler couldn't because he was too frustrated. Tyler tried to pull one over on my dad when he asked if he could bring a friend and his daughter over for a visit.

He asked my dad within the 48-hour time-limit, however, it was agreed in the previous Friend of the Court meeting that little kids were not allowed during the visit. Tyler's friend's child was only 2-years-old.

Tyler came over that day without his friend, but tried to take Madelyne for a walk in her stroller. Once again, there was a heat advisory and my dad did not give Tyler permission. At the end of that particular visit, Tyler must have been suspicious about my whereabouts because he asked my parents where I was. They were evasive and just said that I was busy.

Before Tyler's next visit, my therapist suggested that I spend some time with Tyler at each visit to discuss Madelyne's eating and her play habits. She said that might ease my fears if Tyler was able to get joint custody. At least I could equip Tyler with the basic knowledge of how to take care of Madelyne. I texted Tyler and asked if that was okay. He actually agreed.

He arrived on time for his next visit. I had only planned to stay with him for the first twenty minutes because his dad and step-mom were coming over. I wanted to bring him up-to-date on what Madelyne was eating, what types of toys she was playing with, and her new activities.

I ended up staying in the room for an hour. Tyler chose to sit on the couch and did not participate in anything that I showed him. After an hour, I told him I was leaving. Before I left, however, I told him not to ask my parents about my whereabouts as that was none of his business.

It took him a minute to think about what I was referring to, but once he understood, he was angry.

"What did you just say?" he yelled.

"You heard me." I was walking toward the kitchen.

"I can ask whatever the fuck I want to ask. I deserve to know where you were." He left Madelyne on the floor and came into the kitchen.

My dad was in the family room and came into the kitchen, too. "What's going on?" he asked.

I sighed. "Tyler is being dramatic again."

Tyler was enraged. "You're such a bitch. You like to

ruin every one of my visitations. You're the reason why I don't like coming over here."

"Sure, Tyler." I laughed. "You've missed how many visits? This is the first time I've been home in three months during one of your visits. But go ahead. Blame me because that's what you do. Blame everyone else."

I knew I was goading him, but I just couldn't stop myself. He was so ridiculous.

"I'm leaving," he said as he walked toward the door.

"Oh my God, Tyler. Your parents are coming over. Just calm down and don't ruin their visit."

"They're driving 45 minutes to come over to see Madelyne," my dad chimed in.

Tyler didn't care. He left without saying another word. His parents never came over that day. Tyler missed two of the next four visits.

When he came over for his fifth visit, we exchanged greetings. I wanted to talk with Tyler about some money he owed me.

He made an offer and I made a counter offer. He didn't answer me so I made it again. A heated discussion started.

Both of my parents came into the room. Tyler held Madelyne over a glass coffee table.

"Oh my God!" I screamed. "What the hell are you doing? Put her down! You're going to hurt her!"

"Why?" Tyler asked, laughing. "I'm not the psycho."

Madelyne began crying hysterically and reached out for me. Tears started streaming down my face. "Please, just hand her to my mom. Let's talk. Don't do this."

He began screaming while holding Madelyne over the glass table. "You are such a bad mother! You are a worthless piece of shit!"

My dad went over to Tyler and took Madelyne from him. He took her outside to calm her down.

Meanwhile, Tyler was still screaming. "You know why you divorced me? Because you don't want to live anymore! I'm the best you ever had and no one is going to want you now. You might as well kill yourself!"

My dad came back in and told my mom to take Madelyne and me upstairs. Tyler stood at the bottom of the stairs still yelling disparaging remarks. My dad stood in front of Tyler so he couldn't go upstairs. I told Tyler he couldn't come over for his next visit because he was out of control. My dad finally convinced Tyler to leave without having to call the police.

I texted Tyler before his next visit and reminded him not to come over. I never heard from him so I was suspicious. I had a feeling he was still going to come, so I took my attorney's advice and made sure I was not home. Tyler showed up *and* he brought a friend, which was clearly in violation of the visitation agreement about the 48-hour visitor notice.

Tyler came looking for an argument and he brought

his friend as a witness. When my dad answered the door, he invited both of them in as if nothing had happened. That infuriated Tyler.

"So what happened the other night?" he asked my dad.

"Well, there was some miscommunication but everything is fine now. Hi, Rich," my dad said to Tyler's friend.

"Hi," Rich mumbled. He was clearly embarrassed to even be there.

"I was told not to come over today," said Tyler, who was still looking for *something* to be said in front of Rich.

"Well, you're here." My dad proceeded to tell Tyler the last time Madelyne ate and took a nap. Then he told Tyler and Rich that he would be in the next room if they needed him. My parents and I laughed when they left because Tyler looked like a complete asshole in front of his friend.

҆ৎৎ

Don, my divorce attorney, had not only become like a second father to me during this time, but my mentor as well. He liked to challenge me since I was in law school, so he asked me to write a rough draft of my divorce papers. I had done a lot of thinking since my second stay in the hospital about Tyler's threats of joint custody. I knew the most important thing in the world to Tyler (beside himself) was money. Since Tyler and I had met, Tyler had taken my parents and myself for about $100,000. After I filed for divorce,

Tyler had left me with about $15,000 worth of debt, the majority of it from the hospital co-pay from Madelyne's birth. He decided not to contribute to or pay any of the bills because I was the one who got the anesthesia and surgery so I should have to pay the bills.

Nice, right? So I decided the only way I was going to get Tyler to back off from having joint physical custody was to forgive the money he owed me. So, essentially, I was buying him off.

When I suggested the idea to Don, he was skeptical, but I convinced him to draw up the papers because I knew Tyler was going to take the deal.

A week later I got the e-mail from Don. Tyler bought it—hook, line, and sinker. He still wanted joint legal custody, which meant I had to keep Tyler updated on Madelyne's education, medical issues, and religious instructions. But, I had 100%, sole physical custody. Tyler was only allowed limited parenting time. I was elated. His parenting time schedule was the following:

From 5 months to 12 months:
Each Tuesday and Thursday from 6:00 p.m. to 7:00 p.m. and every Sunday from

12:00 p.m. to 2:00 p.m. at the Plaintiff's home; and Any other time at mutually agreed to by the parties. The defendant may take the child for walks in the stroller. The defendant may bring visitors with 24-hour notice. Visitors shall not exceed two people.

From 12 months to 18 months:
Every Tuesday and Thursday from 6:00 p.m. to 7:00 p.m. and every Sunday from 12:00 p.m. to 5:00 p.m. The Defendant may take the minor child out of the Plaintiff's home for parenting time; and any other time as mutually agreed to by the parties.

Tyler also agreed to an unusual provision that Don and I included in the divorce decree: "There shall be a review of the parenting time schedule when the child reaches the age of 12 months old and when the child reaches the age of 18 months old for an updated parenting time schedule." The reviews would be with our Friend of the Court referee. Tyler had missed so many visits that I was extremely skeptical that he was going to be ready to take Madelyne out when she was a year old.

On September 13, 2010, our divorce was final. Tyler didn't bother to show up to the courthouse. When I got home that night, I contacted Tyler. All of the pent-up frustration from the past four and a half years spilled out into an e-mail:

Now that the papers are signed and the judge has granted the divorce, there are a few things I need to say.

1. I have 100% physical custody of Madelyne. If you show up to this house and disrespect anyone and start an argument, you will be asked to leave. My parents have stepped in and are helping to help raise your child and you will give them the respect they deserve.

2. You are allowed to take Madelyne out in the stroller. There is a 20-minute time limit. If you are not back in time, my dad and I will come looking for you. You will not go to your friend's house.

3. You can invite whom you want to come over on Sunday excluding kids. Twenty-four hours' notice and only two people.

4. If you show up more than 10 minutes late, you are not allowed in. Madelyne has a routine every night and she is not going to be thrown off just because you don't feel like visiting her for the full hour you are allotted. If you don't want to come and visit her, that's

fine. I get the feeling that it's just a chore to you and if you aren't putting any effort into it, it's not worth you coming.

5. I can't force you to do this, but I believe you need help with your anger management. This will affect your relationship with Madelyne later on because if you can't control you anger, I will seek to terminate your parental rights. If you really love your daughter, you need to do this.

You made my life a living hell for four and a half years and today I feel alive for the first time. You will NEVER emotionally abuse me again. You will never make me feel like I am worthless. And again, if I notice that behavior toward Madelyne when she gets older, I will do everything in my power, pay whatever it takes to make sure she does not see you.

If you would like to talk about things calmly, I can do that. Never alone and never outside the house. I will never be alone with you again.

I never received a reply.

Chapter 8

Narcissistic Personality Disorder

I will never forget a conversation Tyler and I had a couple of weeks before I filed for divorce. We were sitting in my car in the driveway of my parents' house, talking about our marriage. I asked him why. Why had he treated me so badly? What did I ever do to him that made him treat me like that?

He looked at me and simply said, "I knew I could treat you as awful as I wanted to because I knew you weren't going to go anywhere."

And he was absolutely right. By that time, he had beaten me down so badly, verbally and emotionally, that I no longer had any self-worth. It felt like he had ripped out my soul and I was just a shell of who I once was.

After I filed for divorce, my therapist, Kate, wanted to delve into my marriage and how I let Tyler completely change me from an independent, outgoing, and vivacious woman to nothing. I wasn't ready to talk about that so, instead, I talked about the court proceedings or my post-partum depression.

I still didn't feel that I was a person worthy of dis-cussion.

Living with my parents was extremely difficult be-cause I made it that way. I took offense to everything they said. If my mom said Madelyne's bath water was too cold, I would take offense and wonder if my mom didn't think I was a good enough mother. If Madelyne spit-up (which all babies do) I felt as if my parents thought I didn't know how to take care of her. If I didn't go to class because I didn't feel well, I thought my parents consid-ered me a failure.

Everything I did, I thought everyone looked at me as if I was worthless because that's how Tyler had made me feel for six years. Then, right before my birthday (Sep-tember), my mom asked me what I wanted. I started cry-ing and said, "I just want to be me again."

When I told Kate at my next session that I was ready to talk about the marriage, she pulled a book entitled *Di-agnostic and Statistical Manual of Mental Disorders – Fourth Edition*, DSM-IV, 1997, American Psychiatric

Association off her shelf. "I want you to listen to this list and at the end, let me know if anything sounds familiar:

"1. Has a grandiose sense of self-importance (e.g. exaggerates achievements and talents, expects to be recognized as superior without commensurate achievements)

"2. Is preoccupied with fantasies of unlimited success, power, brilliance, beauty or ideal love

"3. Requires excessive admiration

"4. Has a sense of entitlement, i.e., unreasonable expectations of especially favorable treatment or automatic compliance with his or her expectations

"5. Is interpersonally exploitative, i.e. takes advantage of others to achieve his or her own ends

"6. Lacks empathy; is unwilling to recognize or identify with the feelings and needs of others

"7. Is often envious of others or believes that others are envious of him or her

"8. Shows arrogant, haughty behaviors, or attitudes."

I was floored after she read the list. Every single item

on that list described Tyler perfectly. When Kate told me that she had just read the symptoms of Narcissistic Personality Disorder (NPD) everything made sense. For the longest time, I used to joke with Tyler that the world didn't revolve around him—a classic sign of a narcissist. I knew Tyler was self-centered but I had no idea that there was an actual disorder that fit him so perfectly. I asked Kate why the other therapists we had seen together didn't pick up on the disorder.

"How often did Tyler go with you?" Kate asked.

I thought for a while. "He only went to a couple of sessions."

"People with NPD are the hardest to treat because they don't think there is anything wrong with them. Do you remember what Tyler said at any of the sessions?"

I laughed. "He thought that he had anger issues because he inherited anger from his dad. Our therapist at the time said you can't inherit behavior."

Kate smiled. "And what did you think?"

I laughed again. "Well, I didn't laugh out loud, of course, but I thought it was one of the most ridiculous things I had ever heard."

"What else does he blame on his parents?" Kate inquired.

"Everything!" I exclaimed. "If you ask him, he had the worst childhood ever."

"What do you think?"

"I honestly don't know because I've never heard the entire story. His mom isn't my favorite person and I can't stand his dad, but Tyler made some pretty bad choices growing up. He dropped out of high school his junior year. He got into drugs. I think he called his mom a whore at some point. He used to smoke pot with his dad." I looked at Kate. "I think he was given a decent shot and he made poor choices."

"A classic sign of someone with NPD is that he will blame everyone else in his life for his problems rather than take responsibility. Everything is always someone else's fault," Kate said.

"Oh yeah," I agreed. "His first marriage broke apart because his ex-wife was a bitch. His engagement broke apart because his ex-fiancée was a bitch. Our marriage broke apart because I'm a bitch. That's the story of his life. Everyone else is to blame."

Kate and I had many conversations about NPD, but after I left therapy, I still had questions: mainly about how I got caught up in that behavior, why I didn't see it right away, and why it took me so long to leave Tyler.

I did my own research and I came across what I called my "NPD Bible."

It's a wonderful book titled, *The Wizard of Oz and Other Narcissists* by Eleanor D. Payson, M.S.W., 2002, Julian Day Publications.

Ms. Payson lists fourteen questions to ask yourself to

find out how *you* are affected by being in a relationship with a person who has NPD:

1. Do you frequently feel as if you exist to listen to or admire his or her special talents and sensitivities?

2. Do you frequently feel hurt or annoyed that you do not get your turn, and if you do, the interest and quality of attention is significantly less than the kid of attention you give?

3. Do you sense an intense degree of pride in this person or feel reluctant to offer your opinions when you know they will differ from his or hers?

4. Do you often feel that the quality of your whole interaction will depend upon the kind of mood he or she is in?

5. Do you feel controlled by this person?

6. Are you afraid of upsetting him for fear of being cut off or retaliated against?

7. Do you have difficulty saying no?

8. Are you exhausted from the kind of energy drain or worry that this relationship causes you?

9. Have you begun to feel lonely in the relationship?

10. Do you often wonder where you stand in the relationship?

11. Are you in constant doubt about what's real?

12. Are you reluctant to let go of this relationship due to a strong sense of protectiveness?

13. Are you staying in the relationship because of your investment of time and energy?

14. Do you stay because you say to yourself the devil you know is better than the devil you don't know?

I answered "yes" to every single one of these questions. My life absolutely centered around Tyler. I never knew what mood he would be in day-to-day. If he came home from work in a bad mood, then I sure as hell better not be happy. If I had an opinion that differed from his, I knew to keep it to myself. I was so exhausted from the constant worry and stress that I would screw up and get berated again and again, my doctor began prescribing sleeping pills a year into our marriage.

Even when we first started dating, there was drama because of Jess and Natalie (Tyler's ex) being friends. Jess and her friends were so angry with me because they thought I was breaking the "girl code" when I started dating Tyler. I didn't understand why they were so upset because Natalie had broken up with him. (Many years later, she and I are now good friends and even go up north every year for a spa weekend.)

Jess and I had never argued before and it was devastating for both of us to be at odds with each other. I wondered if Tyler was really worth all of this drama, but he made me feel special. We opened up to each other. I felt comfortable with him and I just wanted to be with him all the time. I had never felt that way before with anyone but that is exactly how the NPD person wants you to feel. Ms. Payson describes the initial romantic relationship with a NPD person as the following:

> "The NPD individual is often the pursuer with an ardent intent to capture you. You may literally be swept off your feet by his adoration and intensity. This will be followed by a subtle or not so subtle 'turning of the tables' once the relationship is secured. The NPD person's increasing dissatisfaction with you just as you are risking significant emotional investment can be painful and baffling."

Turning the tables is exactly what happened. After enduring weeks of the silent treatment from Jessica's friends when they came to our house, or avoiding the topic of "Tyler" with Jessica, I finally threw all my emotions into the pool and took the plunge. I told Tyler I was in love with him. I expected to hear him say he loved me, but he didn't. He said, "Thanks" and we watched Harry Potter. Awesome.

When he came over my house the next night, he seemed troubled. I asked him if anything was wrong and he said that he had been thinking and he didn't know if I was worth it.

"But I love you!" I cried.

"I'm just tired of the drama," he said to me as I was sobbing.

"But you're not the one who even has to deal with it! How can you do this?"

I was literally begging him to reconsider. In just a matter of weeks, this man had me almost on my knees begging him to see that I was worth it. He left that night and said he would call when he had made his decision. I was a mess. I called in sick to work because I could barely get out of bed. It was ridiculous! I had *never* let a man turn me into this weepy hysterical crybaby before, so what was so special about Tyler? A couple of days later, he invited me over to his house. Right before he turned on a movie, he leaned over and said he loved me. Just like that. And just like that, all the pain of the last couple of days melted away. He loved me! He decided I was worth it after all!

According to *The Wizard of Oz and Other Narcissists,* Eleanor D. Payson, M.S.W., 2002, Julian Day Publications, another skill (if that's what you want to call it) of someone with NPD is that they can take a person's vulnerabilities and manipulate them to achieve guilt or intimidation. For example, Tyler knew I felt very vulnerable when it came to my anxiety disorder. For a long time, I hated my anxiety and tried ignoring the panic attacks which, of course, just made the anxiety worse. I hated that, for 10 years, I had to carry Xanax with me in case I had a panic attack.

If we were out someplace and I said something that made Tyler mad, he would come back with, "Are you going to have a panic attack now?" Or "Do you need to take a Xanax because you're crazy?"

Very rarely did I have to cancel something because I was feeling anxious. However, after the one and only time I did that (early in our marriage) Tyler threw my anxiety in my face like nobody's business. If I was tired and didn't want to go out to dinner, it was because of my anxiety.

If Tyler wanted to go downtown to see a baseball game, but I didn't feel like going, it was because of my anxiety, not because we couldn't afford the tickets.

Tyler even started using my anxiety as an excuse to his friends and family when *he* didn't feel like going out with them. He used my anxiety as an excuse so often that

I began to feel that my anxiety was becoming a problem again, and it hadn't been a problem in over seven years.

When we did go out and I felt a little anxious, I used to be able to count on Tyler to help calm me down. After a while, I was afraid to tell him, which obviously made the anxiety worse. When I met him, I was on the lowest dose of Zoloft (10 mg) to control my anxiety. After the divorce was final, I was taking 100 mg of Zoloft, 60 mg of Cymbalta, and 100 mg of Seroquel a day to fight my anxiety (and post-partum depression).

I used to tell Tyler that he never could understand something unless it happened to him. It used to frustrate me to no end because this lack of understanding or caring was just something I had never encountered before. I learned later on, however, that empathy is *the* biggest ability that an NPD lacks. (*The Wizard of Oz and Other Narcissists,* Eleanor D. Payson, M.S.W., 2002, Julian Day Publications.)

That explained Tyler's behavior after my Grandmother's funeral. He didn't know how I felt because he couldn't empathize with me. Therefore, my emotions of grief were completely foreign to him. Also, our family is extremely close and he used to make fun of us by making lewd comments to me such as maybe we were "too close."

His family had been torn apart, mother and brother against father and brother, and so any feeling of family bonding was totally incomprehensible to him. He saw my parents as a paycheck and nothing more.

The biggest question I kept asking myself after the therapy was why I stayed with Tyler as long as I did. I knew I wasn't in love with him anymore a year into our marriage, but I stayed an extra three years, and I even had a baby with him! I found the best explanation in Ms. Payson's book: The NPD partner makes you feel, "that since YOU are the one who feels unhappy with the relationship, YOU must be the one with the real problem. Or, perhaps you believe him when he convinces you that you can work it out together, despite a pattern of short-lived 'good' behavior followed by a return to business as usual."

This pattern is exactly how I was manipulated into staying with Tyler. We would go through spurts of promised good-behavior at least every month and, of course, it never lasted. Tyler had what was often described as an NPD's "extraordinarily intense verbal attack that knows no bounds...an explosive hot rage which is unmistakably different from the anger expressed by a person who is capable of empathy." (*The Wizard of Oz and Other Narcissists,* Eleanor D. Payson, M.S.W., 2002, Julian Day Publications.)

I would either walk away and take a couple of sleeping pills so I could pass out for the night or I would leave and get a hotel room. Then the next day when I got home from class, he would give me a card expressing how sorry he was and usually my favorite lotion or candy would be on the bed. Then we would talk and Tyler would promise to go to more NA meetings (his form of therapy) or he would try to work on his anger. This "good behavior" would last approximately two weeks before he would become lax and I would start to walk on eggshells again with the cycle repeating itself. And that was my life for six years. I had reached the "Emotional Hostage" stage:

> "Your fear of the NPD individual's rage, along with your fear of his disregard or rejection, may paralyze you from acting on your behalf to get outside help. At this point, your self-esteem is at an all-time low and you are probably questioning your own mental health." (*The Wizard of Oz and Other Narcissists,* Eleanor D. Payson, M.S.W., 2002, Julian Day Publications.)

I tried to help Tyler. I gave him so many chances. In the end, I had to leave. I had to risk the consequences. I knew Tyler would *never* forgive me for filing for divorce. He thought I would never leave him. When the divorce was final, I felt only a slight sense of relief. Tyler hated that he had lost control over me, but he knew my Achilles heel.

Madelyne.

And he would do everything is his power to try to gain that control back, even if it meant using his own daughter as a pawn.

Chapter 9

Sense of Entitlement

Madelyne's first birthday was fast approaching and Tyler and I had to schedule a one-year review with the Friend of the Court per our divorce decree. The night I called to Tyler to remind him of the review, we actually had our first civil conversation in months.

"I want to take her to my house, but I'm scared because I don't know what to do," Tyler admitted.

I breathed a sigh of relief. "I totally understand, Tyler. I felt the same way after she was first born."

We both agreed to wait until after the holidays before Tyler would take Madelyne out of the house. We agreed that Tyler would start slow. He would take Madelyne to the local mall for about an hour. I would even go with him if he asked. Tyler thought it was a good idea. I also suggested that either my dad or myself would spend 5-10 minutes with him each visit to answer any questions about Madelyne. Tyler asked what kind of questions he should ask. I gave him a sample: Did he know her schedule? Did he know her naptimes? Did he know what to feed her? Where would he put her down for a nap when he took her to his house? What time did she go to bed? What was her favorite toy? What time did she eat lunch and dinner? Did he know what to take in a diaper bag?

Tyler didn't know the answer to any of these questions. He admitted again that he was not ready to take care of her by himself.

Madelyne's first birthday was on a Friday night. Tyler and I agreed to have separate celebrations since she was too young to understand what was going on anyway. Since our extended family celebrated her birthday at Thanksgiving, my parents and I just had a little celebration with cake and some presents.

For Tyler's Sunday visit after Madelyne's birthday, he brought his dad and step-mom. They brought cake and presents. I talked with his dad and step-mom for a little while when they first arrived. We all got along and it was a pleasant conversation. I felt happy about the progress of visitation.

All we had to do now was schedule the one-year review with our Friend of the Court referee.

That night, I received a text from Tyler. He said that he was going to take Madelyne to the mall on Tuesday and Thursday nights from now on and to his house on Sunday. He told me to prepare a diaper bag.

I thought, *You have got to be kidding me. What happened during the four hours in between his visitation and the text message?* I had thought we were on the same page. What happened to our conversation about taking it slow? I texted him back and said that he couldn't take her anywhere until we had the review. Also, because I didn't want any confrontations, I cancelled his visitations for the upcoming week. I didn't hear back from him.

That Tuesday, I again informed Tyler that his visitation was cancelled because of his threat to take Madelyne from our house. Tyler came anyway. He rang the doorbell for fifteen minutes and pounded on the door. We didn't answer the door. He went to his car and sat in the driveway for twenty-five minutes. He finally left forty minutes after he arrived.

Two days later, he texted me to say he was going to come Thursday and Sunday to take Madelyne out of the house. He said that his attorney told him that *I* was violating the divorce decree and Tyler had every right to take Madelyne out of the house. He said he was going to take Madelyne out of the house "one way or another."

I'd had enough of Tyler's immaturity. My dad and I went to Don's office to figure out what legal steps to take to stop this insanity. Don told us to file a police report while he contacted Tyler's attorney.

My dad and I went to the police station where I filed a report. The police officer said he was going to contact Tyler to get his side of the story. Did I want him to call me after he talked to Tyler and inform me of what Tyler was going to do regarding the next visit? I said yes.

It wasn't too long after I got home that the police officer called. Tyler told the police officer that he never made any threats to take Madelyne out of the house. Tyler said that he had a court order to take Madelyne out of my house but that I wasn't honoring it. He said that his attorney told him to keep going over to my house so there was a police record of each visit. The police officer advised Tyler that I didn't want him to return to the house. Tyler told the officer that he had an appointment with his attorney that day to discuss the matter. The police officer advised Tyler to only ring the doorbell once and leave.

Meanwhile, Don hadn't been able to contact Tyler's attorney so he sent a fax over to his office stating the following:

> Dear xxxxx:
> I am not sure if you represent Tyler any longer, but his conduct is bordering upon the

necessity of obtaining a personal protection order. There are several incidents that have occurred during his parenting time where his aggressive behavior, in my opinion, would warrant one. There have been numerous threats and actions by him that truly are serious.

I am doing a courtesy of writing this letter to you so that you may intercede and warn him that such behavior will not be tolerated.

As you know, a personal protection order is very detrimental to his parenting time and involvement with his child.

If you no longer represent him, please advise accordingly.

From the time I filed the police report to when we went to court to resolve the matter, we had to call the police eight times. The details of those visits are recorded below:

December 8, 2011: Tyler showed up again. He arrived with another adult. He rang the doorbell repeatedly and pounded on the door. I called the police. Upon their arrival, Tyler told the police that I was not allowing him to take his daughter out of the house. He said he brought a witness per his attorney's instructions. When the police spoke to me, I told them that I didn't mind if Tyler wanted to come into the house to visit with his daughter. Tyler refused. The police escorted him off the property.

December 11, 2011: Tyler arrived with his dad. I answered the door before Tyler could even ring the doorbell. I asked if Tyler was here to visit his daughter. He responded by saying he was going to take her from the house. I closed and locked the door. Tyler began to ring the doorbell and pound on the door. My dad opened the door and asked Tyler the same question. Tyler responded again that he intended to take Madelyne out of the house. My dad closed the door, locked it, and called 9-1-1. Tyler stepped off the porch and walked up to the front window where my mom was changing Madelyne's diaper. He pounded on the window and waved to my mom like a smart ass.

Two police officers arrived. I told them that I was agreeable to let Tyler inside to visit Madelyne per the divorce decree but Tyler refused and wanted to take Madelyne from the house for which he did not have permission. The officer then stated that because Tyler was giving the police officers attitude, that it was probably best not to let him in the house that day. The police officers walked Tyler to his car. Shortly after, Tyler drove away. The police car drove down our street several times to ensure that Tyler had left.

December 12, 2011: I received an e-mail from Tyler that stated:

I have been advised by my attorney not to speak to you until we go back to court do to all the false reports. please do not text or call me unless it is something that I need to know for Maddy. I will be showing up for all my visits with someone else with me as a witness per my attorneys advise. Stop with all the threats, you do not scare me Megan. I have not broken any laws. I am only looking forward to what the papers say I can and that is take my daughter out of your parents house. Have a good day. (Tyler had terrible spelling and grammar, so I didn't change anything in any of his e-mails, texts or letters.)

That same afternoon, Don sent me a letter he received from Tyler's attorney:

This will acknowledge receipt of your correspondence dated December 8, 2011 in the above matter. Please be advised that I do not currently represent Tyler in this matter, however, as a courtesy I will forward a copy of your correspondence to him.

In other words, Tyler had lied to my dad and me and

the police when he said he kept coming over on the "advice of his attorney." He didn't have an attorney.

December 13, 2011: Tyler came with a friend. They sat in the car for approximately ten minutes before coming to the door. My dad opened the door and invited them in for a visit. Tyler screamed that he was there for his daughter and that we were denying his rights. My dad stated three more times that Tyler and his friend could come in and visit, but Tyler screamed even louder that he was being denied his parental rights. My dad closed the door and called 9-1-1. While waiting for the police, Tyler once again knocked on the front window and waved.

The police officer advised Tyler that it would be in his best interests to contact the police department prior to going up to the house and request a peace officer to accompany him to the door. This would prevent any type of false allegations of threatening behavior or the possibility of a domestic incident taking place.

The police officer then came into the house and put it more bluntly to my dad and me. His lieutenant had told his police officers to stop coming over to our house to deal with this problem three times a week because it was a waste of time and resources.

I couldn't have agreed more. The officer explained the peace officer procedure and told us not to open the door if Tyler showed up without a peace officer present. (A peace officer is usually a retired police officer. He can't issue warrants or make arrests. He's sort of like a mediator.)

December 15, 2011: A police car arrived at 6:25 p.m. in front of our house. Tyler arrived at 6:30 p.m. Tyler and two peace officers came to the front door. My dad opened the door and invited Tyler in for his visitation. Tyler stated he was there to take Madelyne out of the house. My dad said he couldn't because he didn't have a court order. Tyler left. One of the officers gave my dad a piece of paper with the case number.

December 20, 2011: Tyler arrived with another adult in the car. Though the police told me not to answer the door unless Tyler was accompanied by a peace officer, because it was the Christmas season, I answered the door and invited Tyler to come inside to visit with his daughter. Tyler said he came to take Madelyne from the house. I said no and closed the door. He left.

December 22, 2011: Don received a Motion Regarding Parenting Time filed by Tyler's attorney. (Apparently, he rehired his old attorney to represent him again.) Tyler had filed seven complaints against me with Friend of the Court. They all stated the same thing: I wouldn't let him take his daughter out of the house, I did whatever I wanted, and I told him that he did not have parental rights.

My attorney answered this motion by simply stating that the divorce decree stated that there was to be a review of parenting time when Madelyne turned twelve months old. The hearing to argue the motion was set for January 18, 2012.

Christmas, 2011: Tyler contacted me around 1:00 p.m. to state he was coming to take Madelyne out of the house. I told him no but, because it was Christmas, he should come over and visit Madelyne. Tyler didn't show.

New Year's Day, 2012: Tyler arrived at noon with another adult. He was not accompanied by a peace officer. When he walked up to the sidewalk, he saw me and my mom sitting on the couch in front of the window. He mouthed to us that he was coming to take Madelyne out of the house. I shook my head no. He turned around and left.

January 3, 2012: Tyler came to the door without a peace officer. Again, even though I was told not to answer the door without a peace officer present, I answered it anyway and begged Tyler to come and see in and see Madelyne. It had been over a month since he had last seen her. Tyler was adamant about taking her out of the house. So I tried a different tactic. I asked him if he had a diaper bag. He said yes. (He was lying.) I asked him if the bag was full of diapers. He said yes. (He was lying.) I asked him what size diaper Madelyne wore. He didn't answer. I asked him if he knew that the temperature was below freezing and there was a wind chill factor in effect for the night.

He didn't answer. I think I made my point because he left.

January fifth, eighth, tenth, twelfth, and fifteenth: He arrived without a peace officer. He rang the doorbell and pounded on the door.

When no one answered, he left.

On January 18, 2012, we all convened in the courthouse for the Motion for Parenting Time hearing. My dad and I arrived with my attorney, but Tyler loved an audience so he brought his dad, step-mom, and his new on-again off-again girlfriend, Heather.

Tyler walked in with his posse in tow, cocky as hell. It took all of two minutes for the judge to knock him off his feet.

The Judge addressed our respective attorneys. "Why are we here?"

"Your honor," Tyler's attorney began, "my client has clearly been denied his parenti—"

The Judge didn't even let him finish. "How?" She turned to my attorney. "Don?"

"Your honor, as you can see in the divorce decree, there was supposed to be a review when the minor child turned twelve-months-old. The Defendant has ignored that review."

"I—if I may, your honor," Tyler's attorney sputtered.

"I see the review in the decree. It's here in black and white," she told Tyler's attorney. "What is the problem?

Why didn't you understand the review? Your client signed the divorce decree."

Tyler's attorney tried again. "But, your honor—"

The judge cut him off. "There is to be a review conducted by the Friend of the Court referee assigned to the parties. Until then, the Defendant will continue his parenting time schedule as agreed upon in the divorce decree. Dismissed."

And that was it. After eight police reports and numerous harassing text messages, phone calls, and e-mails, we won. As Don and Tyler's attorney went to speak with the clerk to file the necessary paperwork, Don told us to wait for him outside the courtroom.

As we exited the courtroom, the hallway was so packed with people that my dad and I were only able to find enough space to lean against the wall. We were talking about the court proceedings when we looked up at saw Tyler and his new girlfriend standing right across from us.

"Why do you lie about everything?" Tyler screamed.

Heather walked up to me and stood about an inch from my face. "As a mother myself, you should be happy that Tyler is the father of your child."

My jaw dropped. "I'm sorry but I don't know you."

She smirked. "Well you're going to get to know me, bitch."

Tyler made a big show of pulling her from me like I

was going to punch her or something. By this time, everyone in the hallway was watching us. We were pure entertainment.

Heather continued her rant. "Two times in the psych ward, Megan? What a great mother you are."

"Where is your mom, the real mother of our child?" Tyler screamed. "She's the one who takes care of Madelyne."

My dad and I tried to move away from Tyler and Heather but they followed us.

"Awww…" Heather mocked. "Do you have to take a Xanax because of your anxiety?"

"Go take your Xanax and sleeping pills, you drug addict," Tyler shouted.

Finally, Don emerged from the courtroom and pulled us into a quiet corridor. He explained that I needed to call our referee to set-up a meeting to discuss a visitation schedule. I told Don about the verbal assault by Tyler and Heather.

Don said he would call Tyler's attorney to let him know that Heather would not be allowed in my house.

Upon leaving the courthouse, Heather screamed, "See you on Sunday, Megan."

I turned toward her and said calmly, "I don't know you, but you are *not* welcome in my home."

That night, Tyler sent me multiple texts attacking my mothering skills, my supposed drug addictions, how he

was going to fight for joint custody of Madelyne, how
Heather would be accompanying him for his visitations,
and a barrage of other insults:

- "Get a life already"
- "Don't you have something better to
do than wasting your parents' money?"
- "Go take your pills and relax, oh
yeah, then your parents would have to watch
our daughter. Oh yeah, they already do."
- "Go talk to your friends. Oh yeah,
you don't have any because of how crazy you
are."
- "Interesting to know you've been to
the hospital a couple of times. You really
need to get it together."
- "Better go call your lawyer and
make up some more stuff about me."
- "Don't be mad at your sorry life."
- "I am sure living with Mom and Dad
the rest of your life will be fun."
- "When you get a job, then you can
pay me child support. Fun."

I finally had to turn my phone off at midnight.

Three weeks after the court date, I hadn't heard from
Tyler despite e-mailing and texting him at ask if he was

coming over to see Madelyne. Finally, I received a letter in the mail addressed in Tyler's handwriting. It said:

This letter is being sent to my attorney, Megan Cyrulewski my ex-wife and our family referee for the friend of the court. I spent the last year having to visit my daughter in my ex-wife's parent's house. For most of the year I was not allowed to even take my daughter for a walk outside of the home. There were also times when my ex-father-in-law for no reason would supervise me in the living room.

My parents and I had to celebrate my daughters first birthday in there living room. If I add up the time that I was allowed to spend with my daughter in the first year of her life it comes out to approximately 8.6 days. How is this fair? I was supposed to be allowed to take my daughter out of the house after she turned a year old. This has not happened and we will be going back to the friend of the court soon to be hopefully put an end to this.

I am supposed to be allowed to bring someone with me for my visits as long as I give 24-hrs notice. The person whom is able to come with me is not being allowed in the home. My ex-wife has now gone to the police with her father and told them I have threatened to kill her and kidnap my daughter. They have continuously made up false accusations about me even with witnesses present. Megan has also said that my visits will be supervised in there home. So I have to sit in a living room with a woman who has said that I am going to kill her and kidnap my daughter and that is supposed to be a healthy environment that I can build a relationship with my daughter?

I love my daughter more than anything in the world and I have help up to my end of the bargain so far, but I will no longer put myself in an environment were people are going to make false accusations about me and jeopardize my relationship with my daughter. No one should be made to have to put up with this sort of treatment. I am working man who pays his child support, who provides medical insurance for his daughter and who has all the means necessary to take care of his child.

I have continuously been threatened that I will have my parental rights removed that my daughter's last name is going to be changed and that I have no say in her life because my ex has 100% physical custody. I have been told that I will have no holidays also. I have text messages and voice mails that support all of this. The drama needs to stop and I need to start building a relationship with my daughter outside of that toxic environment. I am not a criminal; I am a father who wants to be in his daughter's life.

P.S. I just want this letter on file please

To this day, I have no idea what Tyler was trying to accomplish with this letter. Notice how Tyler never mentioned Madelyne by her name throughout the entire letter? He calls her "my daughter," because that is all Madelyne was and always will be to him.

A possession.

Also, Tyler wrote this letter without knowing that for the past year, we had been keeping a visitation log per our attorney's instructions.

If he knew what was in that log, I don't think he would have ever written that letter trying to tout himself as father of the year.

Over the course of a year, Tyler had 108 visitation days. He missed 52.

So this man, who tried to come across as a loving father who was being unjustly persecuted by me, my parents, and the system only spent 48% of his allowed parenting time with his daughter—the "daughter he loved more than anything in the world."

Chapter 10

It's Not About You

On February 7, 2011, we had our Friend of the Court meeting to put forth a recommendation of parenting time to the court. I had my game face on that day. I had had enough of Tyler's games. He tried to manipulate the police into letting him take Madelyne out of our house when that was in clear violation of the court order.

When that didn't work, he *still* came to our house throughout December with the sole purpose of harassing my family.

He dragged me into court to try to prove that I was violating a court order, when in fact, the judge shot him in down in record time. He made himself look like a fool and there were consequences for that. And now he had to pay.

When I first discussed a visitation schedule with Don, he was honest with me and said that I would be *lucky* if I could get Madelyne to 6 months of age before Tyler was allowed to take her out of the house.

When we signed the divorce papers, I was satisfied that I was able to push that back to a year. Now, after watching Tyler screw himself over, I wanted Madelyne to be at least 18 months old before Tyler could take her out of the house and I didn't care what I had to do to get her there.

I knew that if I could get her to 18 months, she would be able to cry as her way of communicating that something was wrong.

And because I knew Tyler so well, I knew it was only a matter of time before he did something to terrify Madelyne.

I knew Tyler was never going to compromise because he was used to getting his way. My strategy was to make it seem like Tyler would get his way, but ultimately the agreement that we reached would be mine. My mindset the day of the Friend of the Court meeting was 18 months or bust.

I arrived at Friend of the Court before Tyler. I called Charlotte's (our referee's) office from the lobby. She told me to tell Tyler to call her office and then she would come and get us. When Tyler arrived, I passed on the message. He completely ignored me.

As soon as we sat down in Charlotte's office, Tyler went off. "I haven't been able to take my daughter out of my in-laws house since the day she was born. My ex-wife thinks she has all the control. I have tried to be a father to my child and I can't even do that. We shouldn't even have to be here today."

Where the hell did I put my violin? I thought to myself. "I" this and "I" that. *Lord give me the strength to get through this meeting without landing myself in jail.*

"Tyler, you signed the divorce papers agreeing to see Madelyne at my parents' house until she was a year old. No one forced you to sign those papers. You also signed the review clause. You knew we were supposed to have a review."

"Actually," Charlotte chimed in, "I have never heard of a review clause either."

Tyler looked at me with a smirk on his face as if to say, "See? Even the Friend of the Court referee agrees with me."

I, on the other hand, felt kind of proud because Don and I were pretty clever to put that review clause in the papers and the judge ruled in our favor.

"So what are the options here?" I asked Charlotte. "Because he's not taking Madelyne out of the house without some type of supervised visitation. He doesn't even know her."

"Whose fault is that?" Tyler yelled.

Charlotte had the patience of a saint. "Let's figure out what we can do from this point forward. What's past is past." She looked at me. "What do you propose?"

This was my opening. Madelyne would turn 18 months on June second. I had to get what I wanted but make it *seem* like I didn't. "I want Tyler to do six months of supervised visitation."

"That's ridiculous!" Tyler bellowed.

"That does seem a little extreme," Charlotte pointed out.

I knew damn well it was extreme, but I couldn't show my cards. "Six months," I repeated.

Tyler crossed his arms like a little kid having a temper tantrum. "I'm not doing that."

I waited to hear Charlotte's suggestion. "Okay. I think we all agree that Tyler needs supervised visitation because he hasn't seen Madelyne since December. Why don't we go back to what was put in the divorce decree and he comes to your parents' house three days a week?"

"No way." Now I was adamant. "He is not welcome at my parents' house. We had to call the police eight times to have him escorted off the property. That option is not even on the table. No way."

Charlotte tried again. "Why don't we have your dad

bring Madelyne to a location mutually agreed upon to visit Tyler?"

Tyler agreed. "That's fine with me."

I shook my head. "No. That's inconvenient for my dad." Not to mention my dad did not want to spend even five minutes with Tyler. "Supervised visitation at a location deemed appropriate by the court."

"There are a couple of places I can think of that we can try." Charlotte looked at me. "You will have to be responsible for the cost of the visitation."

"That's fine with me."

Tyler piped up. "I'm not doing six months."

Charlotte interceded again. "How about this? Tyler, you missed three months of visitation. Why don't you have three months of 're-acquaintance' supervised parenting time?"

I held my breath. Perfect. Three months would bring us to June. That's all I wanted.

After what seemed an eternity, Tyler answered grudgingly, "Fine."

I blew out the breath I realized I had been holding. "I guess that will work," I said, acting like I conceded.

Charlotte was pleased. "Good!"

I did have a couple of other requests, however. "Based on the lovely performance that Tyler and his girlfriend gave at the last court hearing, I don't want any disparaging remarks made and I don't want any significant others present." I looked on Tyler. "I'm not budging on this at all."

Before another argument ensued, Charlotte stepped in. "I think those are fair requests."

She then proceeded to explain the procedure for the supervised visitation. We both had to meet with the director of the location, HARBOR to discuss what our individual goals were for the supervised visitation. After our respective meetings, the visitations would begin. Charlotte typed up the order, we signed it, and we both went on our merry way, or so I thought.

First the text messages started. Tyler asked how I still liked living with Mommy and Daddy. Who was going to take Madelyne to visitation? Mommy or Daddy? Did I graduate from law school yet or was I too stupid?

Then one day I received a phone call from Heather, Tyler's girlfriend. I hung up before she had the chance to spit out anything other than her name.

I sent Tyler a text that said if she ever called me again, I would take out a PPO on her for harassment. Heather had absolutely nothing to do with Madelyne. She just lived for drama, like Tyler. In fact, she was the female version of Tyler. It was bad enough I had to deal with one Tyler, but two?

The harassment got so bad, my parents convinced me to change my phone number. I'd had the same phone number for ten years. Changing your phone number is a bitch, plain and simple. People write down their phone numbers in so many different places on a weekly basis that I constantly had to update it for months. The day I changed my number, I got an e-mail from Tyler:

> When is Madelyne's next dr. apt? What is her sleep schedule? What and when is she eating? Can you bring some toys she likes? I took my orientation on Friday. Please let me know when you get a chance.

First, I was pretty surprised that he remembered Madelyne's name since he always referred to her as "my daughter." Second, in the entire year he visited her at my parents' house, he asked about her eating habits, sleeping habits, and toys but *never* remembered. My dad and I were constantly having to answer the same questions over and over and over again. Third, after every doctor's appointment, I left him a message asking him to call me back so I could tell him about the appointment.

He never called me back. Not once. I knew he was already polishing his "father of the year" act and I wasn't having any of it. I simply responded that her next appointment was at 18 months. Her sleep schedule and eating schedule was a moot point because by the time he was allowed to take her out it would be completely different. I hadn't met with the director yet because I had strep throat. I also let him know I changed my phone number so if he needed to contact me, he could e-mail or call my parents' landline. Apparently that wasn't the response he wanted to hear because his next e-mail was a little more forceful:

> I need to know the date of the appt. I also need to know what her schedule is right now. I have the right to know these things. We have joint legal custody. I don't care that you think it is moot point, it is not to me. All I am asking for is the answer to a couple simple questions and you cant even do that. Please answer the questions or I will call Charlotte and let her know that you are not complying to what we talked about. I am not here to play games with you. I have given up alot of time not seeing my daughter and I will not put up with it any longer. We will start moving forward one way or another. And no that is not a threat. Just please answer my questions with out any extra drama. Thanks.

Unbeknownst to him, I knew that he was in between attorneys. He fired his last attorney but hadn't gotten a new one yet. So at this point, he was constantly contacting Charlotte using her as his "attorney." I felt sorry for her so I tried to work things out between us so he wouldn't keep clogging up Charlotte's voice mail, but I was so tired of his games, his stupid girlfriend, and his father of the year act. I was tired of him, so I exploded:

> You know what, Tyler? Go ahead and call Charlotte and complain all you want. You have asked my dad and you have asked me before about these things and we answered. I'm sick and tired of answering the same damn questions over and over again. It's not my fault you can't remember what we've told you. There are only so many times I will answer your questions and I've reached that point. And I will tell Charlotte the same thing if she calls me.
>
> As far as I'm concerned, you don't have the right to know anything. You haven't proved yourself a genuine father. You drove all the way to our house every T/TH/S in December to harass us and waited in your car for the police to come, but not ONCE did you ask to come in and see your daughter. And about the environment being hostile so you didn't want to come in? That's bullshit and you know it. It didn't become hostile until you made it that way. So you haven't given

up time to see Madelyne. You voluntarily gave up that time and you have no one to blame but yourself for it because YOU were the one playing games, and you lost.

As for the dr. appt., I don't call until the month of the appt. And since I have 100% PHYSICAL CUSTODY BECAUSE YOU SIGNED IT OVER TO ME IN THE DI-VORCE PAPERS, my parents are taking her to the dr. while I'm in class. You know why? Because I called you in the past about her doctor's appointments and not ONCE did you call me back, especially after her one year appointment. So again, call Charlotte and complain because this is exactly what I would tell her. You wouldn't even know what questions to ask at the doctor because you haven't given a DAMN about it in the past.

I am at my breaking point with you. You write this letter to Charlotte about "poor me" and everyone should feel sorry for you when you are nothing but a fraud. You don't give a shit about Madelyne. You haven't since the day she was born and you know it. You wanted a baby so your mommy would come running back to you and that didn't happen. So you left me with taking care of her full time. You stopped getting up for feedings. You came home from work and went to bed at 7:00 when I only had an hour or so of sleep. Then I move into my parents' house and when you would come over, you would complain about how lonely you were and how you would tell your friends never to have a baby. Yeah—that's the father of my child. One month after having her, telling people you don't recommend parenthood.

When you signed the divorce papers, you made me a single mother. It doesn't matter that I live with my parents. They do the job a "husband" would do. But eventually, I have to move out and take care of Madelyne on my own. So forgive me if I don't answer your questions for the fifth time or feel sorry for you because you chose not to see your daughter for almost three months. YOU were the one who ignored my phone calls when I called to talk about Madelyne. And now all of a sudden you have this girlfriend and you want to prove you're a real father? As far as I'm concerned, you are NOT a real father until you prove yourself because you have had 14 months to do that, and you haven't. You have to have supervised visitation! What does that say about you? That you are a complete bullshitter when you say, "I love my daughter and I miss her." You know what? Fuck you for even SAYING those things because you have NO right. NO RIGHT AT ALL! You just want to take her out and show her off like she's a little puppy. She's a real human be-ing—a part of you that you have IGNORED for 3 months.

I called HARBOR today to set-up my meeting. They haven't called back yet. I am complying with all the court orders as I have been from the start. YOU are the one who has violated numerous court orders and there are consequences for your actions. I'm not going to tell you all about Madelyne. You will have to learn about her yourself because you are the one who left her. And now you want the easy way out. You want me to tell you all about her. Well, forget it. Get to know your daughter on your own during visitation. And then maybe, just maybe, I'll see you more than just her sperm donor. Maybe I'll actually see a genuine father.

And if you want to print this e-mail out and send it to Charlotte, be my guest. I have a million things on my plate right now and you

are just an annoyance because I truly believe
that you are not going through all of this because you want to be a great father. I think
you want to show Madelyne off to your girlfriend like she is a puppy. No real father
abandons his daughter for three months.

Obviously I had some pent-up anger that spilled over
into the above e-mail, however, it felt damn good to finally get it all out. And it must have shocked the hell out of
Tyler because I didn't get a response.

୧᧤୨

The night before my scheduled meeting at HAR-
BOR, I sent Tyler a quick e-mail. I wanted him to know
that I had my meeting the following day and that I was
going to request that I be allowed to sit-in on the first session. Madelyne was at the age where she felt very uncomfortable around strangers and since there were going
to be two strangers in the room (Tyler and the social
worker, Zoe) I wanted her to have at least one person in
the room whom she felt comfortable with. I also wanted
him to be honest with me just once, so I asked him if he
really wanted to have a relationship with Madelyne. I told
him I wasn't going to judge him. I just didn't want him to
waste anyone's time if this was all an act. I asked because

he hadn't asked to see her once since December fourth of the previous year. Even though my parents didn't want him to come over to their house, I invited him anyway because I had always encouraged him to have a relationship with Madelyne. He never took me up on that offer. I just couldn't fathom how a parent could not see their child for over four months.

His response was typical "poor me" Tyler:

> Got your e-mail. I will see Maddy at HARBOR, NOT YOU. This not what WE agreed to. I am not going to let YOU and your parents push me out of MY daughters life. Be HONEST with me, what is YOUR problem? LISTEN TO ME ONE LAST TIME, I am not going anywhere, this is not a game to me. I WILL have a GREAT, LOVING relationship with MY daughter. Have a good night. Give Maddy a kiss for me. This really doesn't have to be this hard. You are only punishing Maddy.

Give Maddy a kiss for me? Was he fucking serious?

> Tyler, you still don't get it. You are never going to be a parent. Me being in the room is not about you or me. It's about Madelyne's

comfort. She is going to be hysterical when she sees you because she is terrified of you and there is going to be another stranger in the room. I have to be in there to comfort her. I have the right to be in the room with her.

My parents and I are not pushing you out of Madelyne's life. You've done a really good job of doing that yourself. My PROBLEM is that you haven't seen her since December 4th and that I have absolutely no trust in your abilities to take care of her.

This is hard because you make it hard. Everything in your family is about drama. Everything has to be about you. When you become a parent, YOU are not number one anymore. You've had 14 months to understand that and you haven't.

I'm not trying to keep you away from Madelyne. I would like her to have a loving relationship with her father. But you have to start understanding that Madelyne is first. You don't have a choice whether or not I'm in the room because I will be in there to comfort her when she becomes hysterical. Do you think I want to be in the same room as you? No. But I have to do what is best for my daughter.

I'm not punishing Madelyne at all. You think that everything that has happened is my fault...which you always thought anyway so why should this be any different? Madelyne isn't being punished at all. She is in a loving, caring, non-abusive environment. If you and I would have stayed together, she would not be the happy little girl she is today. Madelyne has a great life. I'm scared of what she is going to be like when you are able to take her out. Because I will tell you right now, when you are allowed to take her out, and she cries when we meet to exchange her, she is NOT going with you. It's not a matter of IF you lose your temper with her, it's a matter of WHEN. And the only way she can communicate is by crying. You abused me during our marriage and I never thought that would happen. It's only a matter of time when you start abusing Madelyne and when that happens, BELIEVE ME, you will NOT be a part of her life unless you get the help you need.

And don't EVER judge how I am raising my daughter saying things like I'm punishing Madelyne. At least I've been there for her 24/7. Where the fuck have you been? Oh yeah, playing games and writing "poor me" letters to Charlotte. You will never EVER understand that when you are a parent, your child comes first because the world revolves around Tyler and it always will. Madelyne is so smart that she is going to see through your bullshit when she gets older. Don't be surprised if she doesn't want a relationship with YOU because of your temper, narcissism, and the way you bullshit ALL the time.

Even though I still lacked the courage to stand-up to Tyler face-to-face, I was able to express myself for the first time in five years, and it felt damn good. I knew he was saving all of my e-mails, text messages, and voice mails to try to use against me in court one day, but I just didn't care. I made sure I didn't say anything I would regret.

The next day, I had my meeting with the director of HARBOR, Adam. He invited me into a conference room after a brief introduction and tour of the facility. He was polite during the tour but as soon as the actual meeting began, I knew Tyler had sold Adam his story of woe. I, once again, was depicted, as the crazy unreasonable psycho trying to keep Tyler away from his daughter while Tyler was just an innocent man who wanted nothing more than to love his daughter. (Cue the vomiting please.)

"Why do you think Tyler needs supervised visitation?" Adam asked.

I was a little caught off guard. "What do you mean?"

"Well, after talking with Tyler, it sounds like he already had supervised visitation at your parents' house."

"What are you talking about?"

Adam looked me straight in the eyes. "The only visitation he's been allowed to have has been at your parents' house. So it's been supervised."

"No," I corrected. "No one was in the room with him."

Adam started typing on him laptop. "So it was supervised."

"No," I repeated. "No one was in the room with him."

"So it was supervised."

"I'm sorry, do we have a problem here?" I felt the tension in the room.

"I'm just trying to gather all the information."

"Tyler signed the divorce decree. He agreed to the visitations at my parents' house. He agreed to the review clause."

Adam smirked. "I heard about the review clause."

"Well, our judge heard about it too and ruled in my favor so that's why we're here, isn't it?"

Adam continued to type. "So it was supervised at your parents' house."

I smiled. "Sure. If that's what you want to believe."

Adam typed a few more notes and then continued. "Tyler gave me his schedule. The visits are one hour per week and we are open on Saturdays. What days are good for you?"

"I'm pretty open. I can do any day of the week except for Saturday."

Adam stared at me again. "Well, Tyler said that Saturday was the best day for him."

"Good for Tyler." I was livid at this point. "I just told you that five out of the six days you are open are good for me."

"Why are you making this so difficult?" Adam asked.

"I'm not making anything difficult. Saturday is the only day I'm not available. If that doesn't work for you, then I'm just going to call the whole thing off and we will have to figure out something else." I stood up to leave.

Adam let out a labored sigh. "I know Tyler wants to see his daughter."

Yeah, Adam. You're right, I thought to myself. *You know everything about your new best friend Tyler, don't you?*

We finally settled on a day (Friday) and I paid for the first visit. When I left the meeting, I was fuming. I called Tyler and left him a message. I told him that I didn't think HARBOR had Madelyne's best interests in mind and I was going to call Charlotte and try to find another place.

When I got home, however, my parents were able to calm me down enough to reason with me.

"Let's just get this over with," my dad said.

I sighed. "I know. I'm just worried about the social worker. Tyler is going to snow her and make her believe that he is the second coming of Jesus."

"I know, but we know who he really is and someday, so will Madelyne," my mom reminded us.

That night, I received an e-mail from Don. Tyler had hired another attorney, Mr. Hutch. Apparently, he fired his first attorney because he lost the review clause motion. After seeing this new attorney in action a couple of times in court, I knew exactly why Tyler chose him. Without a doubt in my mind, Tyler's new attorney was (and still is) the slimiest, most vile attorney I had ever seen in my entire life. If Tyler was an attorney, he would be Mr. Hutch.

My law school professors always used to tell us that our reputation as attorneys was more important than anything. Reputation meant nothing to this guy. Mr. Hutch could have cared less whom he stepped on, which judge he pissed off or what attorney he badmouthed as long as he got paid. I felt like I need to take a shower just after being in the same courtroom as him. Disgusting.

In his introductory e-mail to Don, Mr. Hutch stated

he had taken over the case and then attached all the e-mails I knew Tyler had been saving.

Mr. Hutch called them, "harsh in tone." Aww. Poor Tyler.

The first month of supervised visitation went pretty well. My parents took Madelyne to HARBOR every Friday because I had class. My dad had to take Madelyne into the visiting room for the first visit because she was a little scared, but after she became familiar with her surroundings, she seemed fine. We did have a female social worker, but she was pleasant to my parents so I didn't see any potential problems...until I received the first progress report. Tyler had snowed her big time. The report was dripping with compliments and how wonderful Tyler was with Madelyne. I seriously laughed out loud after I read it:

> During the first visit, Grandfather remained in the room for approximately ten minutes or less so the child could acclimate to the visit. Madelyne was apprehensive of her surroundings during the first visit, brief tears momentarily, but warmed up to Tyler without any issues. Please note that the apprehension appeared to be more due to the environment and the surroundings of a new place.

Tyler has been appropriate during the visits and has not needed any redirection. Tyler is child focused during the visits. The parenting time was utilized by looking at books, playing with toys, and playing with stuffed animals. Tyler is appropriately affectionate with Madelyne. At times, Madelyne will sit next to Tyler, sit on his lap, or allow to be held. Tyler is soft spoken and appropriate throughout. Madelyne appeared to be comfortable in the parenting room and did not display any resistance. At times, Madelyne needs her diaper changed and Tyler is appropriate during diaper changing. At the end of parenting sessions, Tyler exchanges hugs and kisses. Parenting time was appropriate in a structured and monitored setting.

Wow. Were the visits appropriate because I'm just not sure I'm getting that from the report? I thought, *Lady, this is one hour a week. You don't know him. You don't know Madelyne. Also, she's old enough that she doesn't need her diaper changed every hour. Tyler changed her diaper for show.*

The whole hour was a fucking show, but it must have been a good one because she gave it rave reviews every month.

She was so taken by Tyler that she actually tried to get *me* in trouble with the court!

I told Tyler that we wouldn't be able to make the session on June first. My parents confirmed that with Zoe at a visit a month *prior* to cancelling that date so we would have plenty of time to reschedule a make-up date. Zoe told my parents that I had to call HARBOR and let them know why I had to cancel the visit. I called and left a message. Zoe wrote in her last progress report that I called but that I didn't give a reason as to the cancellation nor did I request a make-up session! So of course, Mr. Hutch sent an e-mail to Don asking why I was trying to make things difficult for his client and so on.

I explained what happened to Don and I didn't hear about it again. Don knew I was resigned to the fact that Tyler was going to have visitation with Madelyne. He also knew that as a law school student, I didn't want to do anything to piss off our judge or Friend of the Court. Actually, Don was having a little fun with my case because in 35 years of practicing law, there were some issues he had never come across before. And it was around this time at every meeting I had with Don, he would ask me, "Why did you marry this guy again?" Or he would turn to my dad and ask, "Why did you let her marry this guy again?"

Communication between Tyler and me was actually good, probably because there was no communication.

There wasn't any need for us to talk to each other so when I received an e-mail from him letting me know he was moving and giving me the new address, I offered to come over and help him childproof the house. I wasn't trying to be nosy. (Okay, maybe a little.)

I just remembered what a pain in the ass it was to childproof a house and thought that two sets of hand would be better than one. Plus, he probably didn't have a clue as to what to do. Tyler obviously thought different because he told me that he didn't need help and he was going to bring pictures to our next Friend of the Court meeting. I offered again stating that it might look good to the Friend of the Court if we did it together. The next thing I know, I'm getting an e-mail from Don who in turn received an e-mail from Mr. Hutch:

Don,

I received an e-mail from my client, which contained an e-mail from your client. She wants to come over to my client's house to make sure it is properly childproofed.

Obviously my client would like to avoid the drama. Further, you can be assured, as the father, his first priority is his daughter's safety. He has already made sure the house if childproofed and there is no need for your client's presence at his home.

Don didn't even say anything in his e-mail to me, which usually means the e-mail is not a big deal. I thought Tyler was an idiot to turn down the offer but it made me wonder what he was hiding. With Tyler, nothing is ever black or white. He's extremely shady so if he didn't want me coming over to his house, there had to be a reason. I figured he was probably moving in with his girlfriend, but I knew he had to disclose that information to Friend of the Court and to me because I was the primary custodial parent. Still, in my gut, something felt off. I had a very funny feeling that something wasn't right.

Chapter 11

Why Does Everything Have to be so Difficult?

June 7, 2012 was the day I had been dreading. This was our Friend of the Court meeting when we would decide on Tyler's visitation schedule and divide the holiday schedule. I knew that Don and I had done everything we could do to protect Madelyne and now I had to let her go.

Honestly, part of me was actually looking forward to having a "day off" once a week and I felt that it was Tyler's turn to know what it's like to take care of a toddler. While I love my child, her temper tantrums border on diva-like behavior and Tyler needed to experience a little taste.

As soon as we sat down, Tyler started with what would become his mantra for the meeting: "All I want is time with my daughter."

"That's why we're here, right?" Charlotte pleaded with me.

"That's right. It's time Tyler began his parenting time." I think I shocked both of them.

"That's all I want. I just want time with my daughter," Tyler repeated.

"Okay," Charlotte said. "Well, usually when the child is 18-months-old, she is already into overnight visits but because this is an unusual case, we have to start slow."

"That's fine," I agreed.

"I just want time with my daughter," Tyler repeated.

Charlotte continued. "We can start out with the first three months. During this time, Tyler gets Madelyne every Saturday or Sunday from 11-7 and every Tuesday night from 5-7. Then in September, Tyler can start taking Madelyne for overnight visits every other weekend."

I smiled even though I was dying inside. "That's fine with me."

"I just want time with my daughter."

Her name is Madelyne, I thought.

"Okay," Charlotte said. "Now we have to talk about holidays."

"I've thought about this a lot," Tyler piped up. "Megan's family celebrates Easter so Megan can have her for Easter. Also, I know what it's like growing up in a divorced family and it was hell on Christmas morning, so I want her to wake up in the same house every morning on Christmas, so Megan can have her Christmas morning too. But I want her on Christmas day from noon until evening."

"I think that's very fair," Charlotte said.

Bullshit! Tyler "giving" me Easter and Christmas morning had absolutely *nothing* to do with being from a divorced family. Tyler never did a goddamn thing without getting some type of benefit in return. He gave me Easter and Christmas morning so he didn't have to play Easter Bunny and Santa Claus because he didn't want to buy presents. Also, I cringed at the way he talked about Madelyne, like we were dividing property. Why he couldn't say her name, I don't know, but every time he said "her" instead of Madelyne, it was like nails on a chalkboard.

So keeping my fake smile, I agreed with a, "That's fine."

Charlotte leaned back in her chair. "I'm really proud of you two. You guys have come really far. I'm happy that we were able to come to an agreement today." She turned to Tyler. "So, Tyler, how do you feel about starting your visitation?"

Tyler pulled some pages from a folder he brought

with him. "I took a toddler class at the local hospital. I'm ready." He handed them to me. "I think that you should take the class, too."

Was he fucking kidding me? Was this a joke? Was he actually sitting there telling me that he knew how to raise a toddler after a two-hour toddler class? And I was supposed to take the class because for the past 18-months I hadn't learned how to raise a toddler? What did he think I was doing for the past 18-months? Instead of saying anything, I blatantly ignored him.

I pulled out my own paperwork. "My dad and I put together a list of Madelyne's favorite toys, books, food, emergency contact numbers, and other miscellaneous things for you to look at." I handed it to him.

He wasn't going to take it until Charlotte said that the list was a good idea, then Tyler agreed and said thanks.

Then came my favorite part of the meeting. Charlotte innocently asked if Tyler had installed any safety protection for Madelyne at his house.

"I did. I bought the knob covers, electrical covers, drawer handles, and a couple of other things I can't remember."

Charlotte turned toward me. "Have you seen his house?"

"No," I replied. "I offered to help him install everything but he didn't want my help."

"I think Megan has a right to see the house," Charlotte said to Tyler. "It isn't fair to ask Megan to drop off her child somewhere that she hasn't seen. Let Megan do a walkthrough when she drops off Madelyne for the first visit so she is satisfied."

I couldn't even look at Tyler because I knew he was fuming. He did not want me over at his house but now he didn't have a choice. "That's fair," he agreed quietly.

I looked at him. "Are you and Heather living together?"

"No," he replied.

"Who is Heather?" Charlotte asked.

"Heather is Tyler's girlfriend. She yelled at me in the courthouse, e-mailed me, texted me, and called me so many times that I had to change my phone number. I really don't want to see her and I don't want her around Madelyne."

"Tyler probably needs to have your new phone number," Charlotte said. "Can you give him your new number if he agrees that Heather doesn't contact you?"

"That's fine," I turned toward Tyler. "But she better not call or text me."

"Okay," Tyler replied.

We finalized the agreement, put it in writing, and signed it. All we needed to do now was let our respective attorneys look over the agreement and get it signed by our judge. Charlotte congratulated us on actually getting along and we left. As soon as we got into the parking lot, Tyler admitted he didn't have any of the safety latches installed so his house might not be ready for the visit on Sunday. I told him that there was going to a visit on Sunday whether he was ready or not.

That Sunday, I loaded Madelyne in the car and brought a bag of toys just in case he didn't have any. When we got there, the "Tyler Show" was on full force. On the front lawn, he bent down to hug and kiss Madelyne for all of his neighbors to see. Like they cared. We went inside and I saw a 700 square foot house with gates blocking access to most of it.

Madelyne could only go in the living room and one bedroom. Tyler was nervous so he was talking a lot. He said he didn't buy the house but was renting it from some guy. Then he started telling me about the guy he was renting it from. I tuned him out. I had plenty of practice with that. I did it the entire time we were married.

I looked around the living room. It might have been a small house, but there was about $10,000 worth of furniture and big boy toys in the living room alone. I knew Tyler's credit was bad because he filed for bankruptcy a few years back so I figured Heather probably got a settlement from her divorce and had good credit.

I took a peek in Madelyne's room. No bed, no toys, and the books he picked out for her? Harry Potter. The kid was 18-months-old. I knew the books weren't for Tyler because he didn't like to read. I was seething. Of course, he bought himself a brand new flat screen TV, a TV stand with a fireplace that started by remote, new couches, a leather ottoman, and new guitars, but he couldn't buy a crib for his daughter? He couldn't buy any toys for her?

I kept wandering around as Madelyne explored and Tyler ran his mouth. I looked at what I dubbed "The Shrine of Madelyne." It was this ridiculously enormous picture frame with about ten or fifteen pictures of Madelyne and a note from Heather that said something about how much she loved him. I looked closer at the pictures. Now I knew why Zoe's reports from HARBOR were so damn impressive. She took pictures of Tyler and Madelyne at every visit, which wasn't allowed. The rest of the pictures were downloaded from my Facebook page. They were all my profile pictures at one time. It was really pathetic.

I also noticed more pictures. The screensaver on the TV were pictures of Tyler and Heather. There was a frame with a love poem on the outside and a picture of them on the inside. Fresh cut flowers on the tables and cookbooks on the bookshelves made me a little suspicious. Twenty minutes into the visit, Tyler hadn't said a word about Heather even though her picture was everywhere.

"Did Heather help you decorate?" I asked.

"She likes fresh flowers. We always have some," he replied.

"Wait a minute. Does she live here?"

"Yeah," he said like it was no big deal.

Breathe in breathe out. I could either go one of two ways. I could snatch Madelyne, run to the car, and figure this out in court or comply with the temporary agreement and call my attorney first thing in the morning. I wasn't about to cause a scene in front of Madelyne, so for the moment, I let it go.

Tyler must have figured that I was fine with Heather living with him because he had the balls to ask me to come half an hour early that evening so I could meet Heather. I had absolutely nothing to say to the psycho but I agreed to come early anyway. Leaving Madelyne with Tyler that day was one of the hardest things I've ever had to do. In fact, I think I would have picked labor all over again rather than leave her there.

When I came back that evening, I almost busted out laughing because Madelyne had caused a tornado in their living room. DVD's, books, cards, and her toys were scattered all over the place.

"Mommy!" Madelyne squealed when I came in the door.

Tyler looked exhausted. "I don't know how you do this every day."

"You only had her for eight hours!" I exclaimed.

Heather was in the kitchen. She was wearing a white T-shirt without a bra and daisy duke shorts. I was glad my daughter was too young to understand how inappropriate that outfit was. I wasn't sure why Heather dressed like that because there wasn't a competition between us for Tyler. She could have him.

"How did it go today?" I asked Tyler.

"Good. She played with her toys." He looked as though he was going to fall asleep any minute.

"Did she take a nap?"

Tyler nodded. "She slept on me for like, two hours."

Right, I thought. She hadn't slept on anyone for two hours since she was a baby.

"They were so adorable!" Heather piped in from the kitchen. "We gave her kiwi and mango with her dinner and she loved it."

Was I in a parallel universe here? Did they actually think that I did not know my child well enough to believe this shit they were shoveling my way? Madelyne was a picky eater and I knew she did not eat kiwi or mango.

"Okay. Well, have a good night." I walked with Madelyne toward the door.

"Bye, Maddy," Heather said. "I love you." Jesus.

"Can Daddy have a hug?" Tyler asked from the couch.

"No," Madelyne said.

I hid my smile. "I think she's pretty tired."

The next morning, I called Don first thing. I explained the situation and he told me to call Charlotte. Charlotte said that she was not aware of the live-in situation and I should call Tyler to ask for Heather's last name so Don could run a background check. When I called Tyler, shit hit the fan.

"What the fuck is this? After one visit, why do you have to stir up drama?" he screamed into the phone.

"You lied to me and you lied to the Friend of the Court! I dropped my daughter off with someone I don't even know! Do you know how hard that was? Do you even get that?"

"Who cares?" Tyler asked. "It doesn't matter anyway because we're getting married."

"Wait. What?" I was shocked. "Well, nine months after the divorce is final, you just can't wait, can you?"

"Whatever, Megan. We're getting married so you don't need to know about her."

I laughed. "You have got to be fucking kidding me. I don't care if you're getting married. That doesn't negate the fact that I don't know a damn thing about her! What's her last name?"

"Same as mine!" He screeched and hung up.

My mom was sitting on the couch across from me. "So…they aren't hiding anything."

"Oh no. Not at all." I sighed. My phone rang. "Hello?"

"Megan? It's Heather."

Oh my God. Not again. I changed my number so she wouldn't call me. Tyler promised me he wouldn't give her my new number. I put her on speaker so my mom could hear. "What is it, Heather?"

She started spelling her last name. "But you can ask me anything you want."

"No offense, Heather, but I don't believe a word that comes out of your mouth."

"Listen, Meg—" she began.

"Don't call me Meg," I said.

It was a knee-jerk reaction and I kicked myself after. Only my close friends call me Meg and to hear my nickname come out her mouth—well, it was a mistake because from that day on, all she called me was Meg.

"Listen, *Meg*," she continued, "you aren't being a very good mother. You are using your daughter to get back at Tyler. I'm a mother myself and I know—"

I hung up on her. I was not about to listen to her rambling on about herself or Tyler. I didn't care what she had to say. I called my attorney and told him to stop drafting the visitation order until we found out just who Heather was and what they were hiding. Don thought there was something fishy, too, so he gave us the number of a private investigator who he had worked with before.

That night as I was getting ready for bed, I got a phone call from a very irate Tyler.

"You called Charlotte and got her involved in this? What is your problem?"

"Of course, I called her. You lied to both of us. This is a huge deal even if you think it's not!"

After he dropped a billion f-bombs and screamed loud enough to probably wake up his neighbors, he finally realized I wasn't backing down. "What do you want, Megan?"

"First, I told you that Heather was not supposed to contact me anymore. Second, if I had known you two were living together, I never would have agreed to overnight visits starting in September. I don't know anything about Heather. I don't trust your capabilities as a parent because it's difficult for me to believe that it was a smooth transition from one hour of supervised visitation to eight hours unsupervised visitation. I think you lied to me on Sunday about her napping and about what she ate. You don't have a bed for her. You don't have any toys for her. This whole situation just makes me extremely uncomfortable. If it was just you, I probably wouldn't be as uncomfortable. But put yourself in my shoes for once."

"So what would make you comfortable?" Tyler asked.

"I think that for the next month, you should have visitation on Sunday from 12-3. Then the hours will increase the second month from 12-5. Then they will increase from 11-7."

To my surprise, Tyler agreed. He also added a couple of suggestions. "Let's hold off on the overnight visits and we will eliminate the weekday visit."

"Okay. If you agree, then I will e-mail my attorney in the morning with the changes and he will draft up a new order and send it to your attorney."

"That works for me," Tyler said.

The next morning, I e-mailed Don with the changes. He was surprised but agreed to draft the new order. Things seemed to calm down for the next couple of days until that Saturday, which was the day before Tyler's second visitation *and* Father's day. Madelyne had received two immunizations a week prior. Her pediatrician told us if she were to have a reaction to these shots, it would be a delayed reaction. Sure enough, she woke up Saturday morning with a fever. And I hated that my first thought was shit because Tyler is going to be pissed off if I cancel Father's Day.

I texted Tyler and told him that it seemed as though Madelyne was having a reaction to the immunizations and she had a slight fever of 99.6. I told him that hopefully I didn't have to cancel the following day, but I just wanted to let him know what was going on. I asked him if he wanted me to keep him posted throughout the day. He didn't answer me. I texted him again around 11:00 that evening stating that Madelyne still had a temperature and that his concern for Madelyne was touching.

He tried calling me but I didn't answer the phone. I quickly texted him to say that I don't answer my phone at night because I don't want to wake up Madelyne. He finally texted me to say that I was a liar and that Madelyne didn't have a fever. I was floored. A barrage of texts went back and forth with me basically calling him an asshole and his girlfriend a piece of white trash. Then he called me and my parents liars and said that we were using Madelyne as a pawn. Then in between the texts, I received an e-mail from Heather:

> Megan it's Heather I figured that you wouldn't open my e-mail so I'm sending this from Tyler's. (Also so it's on record.) If the problem you have is with me thats fine. But stop taking it out on Tyler and using Maddy as a pawn. Tyler's heart is breaking from this tug of war you keep playing. So like I said if the problem is me then I won't be at MY house when Maddy is here till we can come to a resolution. Tyler's dad is expecting to FINALLY see his graddaughter not only is it his birthday but it's fathers day as well on Sunday. I have seen every e-mail and heard everything you have said about me and I really feel I am being more than gracious. I do understand what you are going threw and I

am trying to open the door for communication. Hanging up on me was not very amicable in my eyes. The fact is Tyler and I will be married this week and Maddy will have a step-mom. I will do everything in my power to keep a open door and respect you as Maddy's mom. As another woman I don't right now because of all the ways you have attacked me and hurt Tyler. But we are not the issue here. There is a daughter who needs her father and a father who has been MORE than patient doing things most men would not do, just to try to see his daughter. So I will close with this, I'M NOT GOING ANYWHERE AND NEITHER IS TYLER. I am leaving the door open. Please let Tyler have his visits I won't be here. I PROMISE. I will not go on Sunday either for fathers day. Lets keep moving forward and put Maddy first. She is the one who will ultimately pay the price in the end. (Heather's grammar and spelling are also atrocious so I copied all the messages word for word.)

Why couldn't my ex-husband be with someone who wasn't a complete idiot like himself? Was that too much to ask? I mean, *come on.* So it's on record? What record?

Whose record? What planet were these people on? Who
cared so much about this e-mail that they were going to
include it in some record? By this time, it was midnight
and I had enough. I responded to Heather with a short e-
mail:

> Heather, if you ever contact me again,
> you will be served with a PPO. This is har-
> assment. I could care less that you two are
> getting married. Doesn't surprise me. He
> wants sex and you have credit to buy him
> nice things. How long do you think that will
> last? Why don't you talk to the three other
> women he's married/been engaged to in order
> to find out just who he is? Someone tried to
> warn me once from marrying him. Maybe
> someone needs to do the same with you. As
> far as Madelyne is concerned, you don't need
> to be around when she is at Tyler's house. He
> needs to spend alone time with her, not play-
> ing house with you.

I texted Tyler and told him I would let him know in
the morning if Madelyne still had a fever. Then I turned
off my phone and went to sleep.

The next morning, Madelyne had a temperature of
100.5. She had never had a temperature that high before

so I called her pediatrician. (He was definitely not too happy because it was 8:00 am on Father's Day.) He told me to keep her indoors all day because of the humidity and let her sleep as long as she wanted during her nap times. If she still had a fever the next morning, I was to bring her to the office. I thanked him and texted Tyler the news. I told him to have a good day with his dad and to call me later so I could give him an update on Madelyne. He texted me back. He told me I was a liar, I ruined his father's day on purpose, and that he was filing harassment charges with the police first thing Monday morning for "the nasty text messages" I sent him the previous night. I didn't answer him.

First thing Monday morning, I got a phone call. I didn't answer because it was a number I didn't recognize. It was a detective from the police department calling in regards to a harassment complaint filed against me. I couldn't believe that they had actually followed through on their threat! I called Don who immediately called the police department and took care of it. Apparently the police had a good laugh over the whole thing. But Don did say, "Megan, you've got to stop with the texting."

That's the only time Don ever warned me about anything, so I knew he was serious. Don would be proud to know that I haven't texted Tyler since his stern warning.

Later on that week, Tyler e-mailed me to ask about visitation that coming Sunday. The original plan was that

I would go to his house to drop off and pick up Madelyne. After the texting, e-mailing, and police harassment
charges debacle, I knew I couldn't be alone with him. I
didn't trust him. We also hadn't signed the final parenting
time order, so legally I didn't have to comply with the
temporary order. However, delaying any parenting time
would be detrimental to Madelyne, so any personal feelings I had about Tyler would have to be put on the back
burner.

Let me just say, for anyone that has gone through an
unpleasant divorce and child custody case, that is *not* an
easy thing to do. It was extremely hard to act civil in
front of my child because every time I saw Tyler I shud-
dered in disgust.

Don suggested that we go ahead with the visitation
as scheduled but that we exchange Madelyne in the police parking lot, and that I bring my dad with me just in
case. It was not my first choice, but it was the safest location. I e-mailed Tyler and let him know of the arrange-
ments. When we got there, Tyler had parked so far away
from the police station that we were basically exchanging
Madelyne in a parking lot, which defeated the whole purpose of meeting at a police station in the first place. I
didn't say a word. I took Madelyne out of her car seat,
kissed her on the forehead and handed her to my dad. It
was too much to ask me to hand her to Tyler.

When we picked her up that night, I could see the relief on my dad's face when Tyler handed her over. Tyler didn't say a word to either of us. He got back in his car and sped away.

The next morning, I received an e-mail from Don. He forwarded an e-mail from Tyler's attorney:

> My client never agreed to a new parenting order. He insisted he wants the original Friend of the Court agreement of June 7, 2012. Unfortunately, Ms. Cyrulewski is making this difficult. As a result, I feel it necessary to file a motion to adopt the recommendations.
>
> While I appreciate your forceful advocacy on behalf of your client, I cannot agree to this new order. Tyler has done everything he can to comply with the parties' agreement. Ms. Cyrulewski needs to realize that Tyler will be spending as much time in his journey to share full physical custody of Madelyne.

That motherfucking bastard played me! Tyler was never going to agree to the new order we had discussed. Instead, he made me look like *I* was not complying with the court. I think I was more pissed off at myself than Tyler.

I should have seen this coming, but I never thought

he could be this vindictive. He made me look like a fool and I promised myself that was the *last* time that would ever happen.

Plus, what was this shit about joint custody? Was he out of his mind? He never wanted joint custody! The only way to change that was if I agreed (which was NEVER going to happen) or if we went to trial. Who was he kidding?

I also wondered if Mr. Hatch knew that his client was not asking to take his daughter for the weekday visit. I had e-mailed Tyler every Monday for the past three weeks and asked if he was going to take her that Tuesday as stipulated in the temporary order and he never replied. This didn't seem to me as though his client was "complying with the court order."

Don asked me what I wanted to do. I wasn't ready to sign the other agreement as it stood. I wanted to add some changes:

- Both parties would attend Communication Counseling Sessions.
- The weeknight visitation would be eliminated.
- If Madelyne was ill, visitation would not take place with appropriate confirmation.
- The parties would evenly split the cost of day care and developmental activities

of Madelyne with day care beginning in January.

Tyler, of course, didn't agree to any of the changes. He didn't understand why I would want to keep Madelyne home if she was ill. I thought to myself, as an adult, I like to be home when I'm sick, so why would it be any different for a child? Again, it was Tyler's feeling of entitlement. No one was going to tell him that he couldn't take care of *his* daughter when she was sick. As for day care, when I brought up the topic a while back, he asked why she needed to go since I was in school and living with my parents.

I think his exact words were, "Are you and your parents too lazy to watch her?" Asks the parent who hadn't taken care of her for 18 months. My reasoning was that because she is an only child, she needed the socialization. I enrolled her part-time, so only three days a week. Basically, Tyler didn't want to fork over the money. But he wanted to have joint custody!

The next morning as I was sitting in class, I received an e-mail from Tyler:

We have a court date schedule for Wednesday July 11 at 8:30 am. Call your attorney. He will let you know. *This message was sent from my new awesome i-phone.*

Oh goody. Heather went out and bought him another new toy. My response was:

> This e-mail just reeks of maturity. I like that you can afford a new i-phone, but can't afford a crib for you daughter. Nice. Since it seems like you can afford things now, you should have diapers, wipes, food, a crib, mattress, and extra change of clothes, swimsuit, life jacket, and swimming shoes for Madelyne at your house. My dad and I will see you on Sunday.

Apparently I took it too far because I didn't compliment him on his new toy *and* I asked him to actually spend money on his daughter because he was pretty pissed in his response:

> This is an 8-hour visit. You are supposed to supply diapers and clothes and food. I have spoken to Charlotte about this in the past. Please call her if you don't be leave me. And you should start to read the friend of the court handbook. I will bring this up at court. All you want to do is make things hard. This has nothing to do with money. You are responsible for these items. Keep playing games, Me-

gan, see were it gets you. And no that is not a threat. I am done just sitting on the sidelines while you and you're parents do what ever the hell you feel like doing. You can't even show up to transfer Maddy, again you have to have you're parents handle it. I will not continue to go to the Troy police station in the future to pick my daughter up. You want to paint some picture to the court that I am so bad guy. What a joke. The court sees bad fathers and let me tell you, I am not one of them. Go talk to a mom who really has to struggle and get back with me. See you Sunday. I will get what I need for Maddy since you want to continue to play games with my daughter.

I almost burst out laughing in the middle of class. I could just imagine Tyler bringing this up in court: "Judge, my ex-wife says I have to provide the essentials of life for my daughter but the Friend of the Court handbook says I don't have to. Oh and by the way, I want to petition for joint custody." And just when I thought things couldn't get any more bizarre, another e-mail pops-up on my screen and it's from Heather:

Your behavior borders on unstable. Lets

just call it as it is YOU left Tyler HE MOVE
ON. You live with mommy and daddy you're
jealous and most defiantly still in love with
Tyler. MY family has been warned that if you
contact ANY of them to call the police. I'm
pretty sure you don't want to start a PUBLIC
POLICE paper trail showing your unstability.
I have taken your trash talk and abuse and
I'm not going to anymore. You made your
bed so lie in it. I'm sure mommy will make it
for you in the morning again. God forbid you
ever take any responsibility for any of your
actions. Your a disgrace to single moms who
actually struggle and don't get support, medical and everything else you take for granted.
Like a normal father for your child. My question to you is what have YOU bought Maddy
with YOUR money? Oh that's right YOU
don't have any it's Tyler's and your parents.
Well I've bought her a lot. With money I
MAKE.

Oh ya and about Tyler missing YOU as a
family when you were a family you left two
weeks after having Maddy. And just for your
time line I was there soon after that. Tyler has
a family now a REAL one he has a BEAU-
TIFUL healthy wife a loving step-daughter

who thinks the world of him and is just ap-
palled also by your behavior. She had a real
shit for a father. Tyler actually gets to see
HIS dad and family now that his world
doesn't revolve around your anxiety and selfish behavior. Oh ya and WE WILL get our
time with Maddy.

So enjoy the mess you made of your life
I hope you do some serious soul searching
and change because overtime you try to cause
chaos in our life all you do is bring us closer
together. I want to thank your mom and dad
and you for giving me Tyler. Have a BEAU-
TIFUL DAY. Tyler read this before I sent it
so he knows. This e-mail needs no response.
But the door is open if you ever want to be
amicable. I'm done giving you grace. (that's
an unwarranted favor) and don't come back
at me with your PPO threats and all you other
crazy bull shit you don't scare me. Just move
on already.

I wondered what it was like to live in a house with
two people who were complete morons because living
with one moron drove me into the psych ward. Tyler (and
obviously Heather) truly believed that just because they
said something, everybody was going to believe them.

By this time, our private investigator had found some information about Heather. I thought about putting that information about Heather in this book, but to be honest, Heather isn't even worth discussing. Let me just say this, there is a paper trail with Heather's name on it, leading back through the court system all the way to 1995 and it's not pretty.

Also, to touch upon a topic that Heather kept bringing up, my anxiety had nothing to do with Tyler not seeing his family. Tyler hated spending time with his dad so that's why we never visited him. And anyone who calls themselves BEAUTIFUL in capital letters might be insecure. I'm just saying. Finally, Tyler was not a gift, believe me. But you're welcome, anyway Heather, so enjoy!

I forwarded Heather's e-mail to Don and asked if he could contact Mr. Hutch and please ask that Heather not contact me anymore. I don't have to deal with her, I don't have to talk to her, and I sure as hell don't have to read any more stupid e-mails from her. Don agreed and he did confirm the court date for July 8. He said he really didn't want to go to court over the motion and to reconsider signing the order that was mutually agreed upon at the first meeting on June seventh. My heart sank because I knew Don was right. Even though Heather and Tyler got around the court by getting married after lying about living together, now it was a moot point. The best I could

hope for was that in time, Tyler would figure that taking care of Madelyne would be too hard, and he would start cancelling visits like he used to do.

The next Sunday visitation came and went without any problems. That week, however, was the Fourth of July and, according to the terms of the agreement, Tyler was supposed to have Madelyne from 9 am to 8 pm. He e-mailed me the day before the holiday to ask if I could meet him at the police station at 11 am instead of 9 am. So, I thought, he was already trying to cut back his hours of visitation. I didn't trust him so I told him that I would be there at 9 am because that's what was stated in the agreement.

I knew the day was going to be extremely difficult for him. He just had Madelyne that Sunday for eight hours and now he had her again for eleven hours. She probably wasn't going to take a nap and therefore was going to get pretty cranky toward the evening.

Sure enough, around 7:30 pm, my parents' landline rang. My dad answered the phone and it was Tyler. My dad could hear Madelyne crying in the background. Tyler asked if we could meet him at the police station parking lot because Madelyne was tired. My dad readily agreed.

When we pulled up, Tyler was already there. Our windows were down so we heard Madelyne cry. When we got out and Tyler opened the back door of his car, she stopped crying and smiled at my dad and me. Tyler, who was obviously pissed that he had to admit defeat and bring her back early, started to mock her.

"There's your family," he said to Madelyne as he unbuckled her car seat. "Are you happy now?"

My dad turned and looked at me. I just shook my head. "She's just tired," my dad said.

Tyler handed her over to my dad. "There's your real family. See them? There they are. Now you're not crying, are you?" Then he got back in his car and drove away.

"Am I wrong or did he just mock an 18-month-old?" I asked my dad.

"That was pathetic," my dad said while clutching Madelyne.

We got her home and she gave Grandma a huge hug. The next day, she started doing something she had never done before. She would play, but then she would stop, and point to all of us and say, "Mommy, Grandpa, Grandma," and then continue to play. She did that several times a day. It was as if she was making sure we were still there.

I had a bad feeling in the pit of my stomach. I could feel my anxiety rise the closer it came to the next Sunday for visitation. The night before visitation, after I put Madelyne to bed, I talked to my parents.

"Something happened on the Fourth of July."

"What do you mean?" my mom asked.

"I just know something happened. Tyler's pride

would never have let him bring her back early unless something happened." I insisted.

"What do you think we should do?" my dad asked.

"There's nothing we can do. We have to go to the visitation. I just know something happened. I think he lost his temper and screamed at her. That probably scared her and that's why he wasn't able to calm her down again."

"Maybe you're just overthinking it," my mom said.

"Maybe."

I couldn't sleep that night. I knew my child. I knew my ex-husband. Madelyne never cried. Tyler always screamed.

Something was wrong.

Chapter 12

Hell Hath No Fury Like A Crazy Ex-Husband

The morning of July 8, 2012 I was a nervous wreck. I just had a really bad feeling. My dad and I put Madelyne in the car and drove toward the police station. She was unusually quiet. When we pulled into the parking lot, she started to cry. When I pulled next to Tyler's SUV, she started to scream. Madelyne hardly ever cried and she never screamed.

I got out of the car and went around the back to get Madelyne. Tears streamed down her face. I didn't know what to do. I handed her to my dad but he didn't hand her to Tyler. My dad knew something was wrong, too.

Tyler tried to talk to Madelyne but every time he got

closer to her, she turned her head into my dad's shoulder. Tyler went back to his car and got a purple stuffed bunny. He came back and tried to give it to Madelyne, but she wanted nothing to do with it or him. She reached out for me. I took her and tried to calm her down.

"What's wrong with her?" Tyler asked.

"I don't know." I answered. "Did something happen on Wednesday?"

Tyler rolled his eyes. "Why do you do this?"

I was so exasperated. "Tyler, I'm just trying to figure this out. Did you and Heather have a fight in front of her? Did you yell at her? Did you lose your temper?"

"Babies cry," Tyler snapped.

Before I could even react, he snatched Madelyne out of my arms and put her in the back of his car. She started to hyperventilate.

"What are you doing?" I screamed.

Tyler ignored me as he tried to strap her in the car seat.

"Tyler! She's terrified! You can't do this! Let's take her to a park or something. She has to calm down before she can go with you!" Was he crazy? How could he do this to his own child?

I squeezed in between him and the doorframe of the car door. "Tyler! Stop!"

"Don't touch my fucking car!" Tyler screeched as he tried to slam the door shut. I had my leg in between the door and the frame so he couldn't close the door. I tried reaching Madelyne who was still wailing and howling. It was a horrific sound. All of a sudden, Tyler put me in a chokehold and dragged me from the car. I could see my dad out of the corner of my eye trying to get someone's, anyone's, attention.

"*Help!*" I screamed. "*Help me!*" But we were parked too far away from the actual police station and since it was Sunday, no one was around. "*Someone help me. Please!*"

Tyler tightened his arm around my throat. I couldn't breathe. *Oh my God*, I thought. *He's going to kill me.* Tyler was completely out of control. I knew if I didn't do something soon, I was going to blackout. I began to move around and I managed to wrest myself free. I immediately ran around to the other side of the car while my dad put himself in between the car door and Tyler.

Even though my dad and I had not spoken a word to each other, our common goal was to get Madelyne out of the car and we were going to work together to do that. As I was unbuckling Madelyne I could hear Tyler taunt my dad.

"Where are your balls, Jim?" Tyler laughed. "Letting your daughter run your house. Do you do everything she tells you? Your daughter is breaking the law. She's going to jail."

My dad didn't answer. He watched me to make sure

I had Madelyne. As soon as I had her, I started walking toward the police station.

Tyler walked in front of me and dialed 9-1-1. "My ex-wife just assaulted me," he told the 911 operator. "I want her arrested."

"Get out of my way," I kept telling him because he was taunting me as we walked to the station. "Leave me alone."

Madelyne was still crying.

When we walked into the station, Tyler started yelling that I assaulted him and he wanted me to go to jail. I didn't say a word. The bruises on my body spoke for themselves. I knew Tyler wasn't going home that night. The officer called for backup and asked if I wanted paramedics.

I said yes because I had never seen Madelyne in such a panicked state. She was probably fine, but I wanted her checked to be sure.

By the time my dad came into the station, Tyler was on the phone with Heather. "I can't believe it either, honey. She just assaulted me out of nowhere." Tyler looked up and saw an officer walking toward him. "Here comes Bill now. I'll be home soon. Love you."

He looked at me and smirked. So Tyler knew the police officer. Did he think that was going to erase the fact that he attacked me?

The officers split us up. They took Tyler outside and

talked to me while my dad held Madelyne who had fallen asleep on him.

I told Bill what had happened. At first, he seemed a little cold.

"I have a hard time believing that he would do something like this in a police station parking lot," Bill said.

"Well, I don't know what to tell you, but that's what happened," I replied.

"You know there's video cameras outside that probably recorded the entire episode."

"Good. I hope you watch it." I had forgotten about the cameras. I was glad that the proof was captured on tape!

I showed Bill my bruises and scrapes and he told me to sit and wait while he went outside to talk with Tyler. This was Tyler's handwritten statement before he talked to the officers:

> I showed up at the Troy Police Station at 10:40 am waiting for my ex-wife Megan Cyrulewski and her father Jim Cyrulewski to exchange my daughter for my parenting time from 11:00 am until 7:00 pm. My daughter was a little up set and my ex-wife was trying to take her out of the seat and pushing me away saying she was not going with me. Her father then also pushed me out of the way to

get my daughter out of the car. I then pulled Megan out of the way and tried to shut the door. Megan and her father continued to push me away and then I said we need to call the police.

When Bill told Tyler that the entire episode had been caught on camera, Tyler changed his story and said that he "Pulled Megan away from the car by wrapping my arm around her upper body and walked backward."

After that explanation, Bill told Tyler he was under arrest for domestic violence and assault.

I couldn't hear what Tyler said, but when Bill finally came back inside to tell us that Tyler was going to jail, he told me the gist of what happened. Tyler pretty much exploded. He wanted to know why my dad and I were not being arrested as well. Bill explained that we were the ones who had injuries and Tyler had admitted that he had touched us. Tyler also stated that I was in law school so I knew how to "work the system."

Bill told him that I had not informed anyone in the police station that I was in law school. Tyler stated that I was doing everything I could to prevent him from seeing his daughter. Bill told him that he was under the impression that these visitations were voluntary because a judge had not signed the order yet. (The court date was in three days.)

After two hours we were able to go home. We thanked the officers for their help. They were extremely caring and calm with Madelyne and made the process very smooth for my dad and myself. I had been very upset when I had walked into the station. After Bill realized what had actually happened, he had done his best to calm me down. He did give me a warning about Tyler before I left. "Be careful of this guy. He wants revenge. He is the type of guy who will sit in your driveway for ten minutes scratching his arm and then call the police to say you did it."

And this was from a person who was supposedly Tyler's friend.

When we got home, my mom starting crying when she saw us. Madelyne seemed to be a little clingier, too. We all were in disbelief about what had happened. Other than a few pushes and shoves during our marriage, Tyler had never let his anger become that physical. I believed that the stress of having three visitations in one week was too much for him and he couldn't handle it. But instead of admitting it, he let his anger get the best of him.

I never would have judged him if he had admitted that he was in over his head. During the week when my dad went to work, my mom and I split the day watching Madelyne. It's hard work to keep a toddler entertained all day. All three adults in our household are in bed by 9:30 most nights because we're exhausted. I knew Tyler was not going to be able to handle it. I just thought that the visits would taper off. I never expected something like this. Before we went to bed that night, my dad called Don to let him know what had happened. Since it was Sunday, it was a brief conversation. Don's primary concern was that everyone was fine and nobody was seriously hurt. My dad assured him that, under the circumstances, we were fine and we would talk to him soon.

Don called the day before the scheduled court hearing (to adopt the parenting time schedule). He asked if I was ready for the next day.

"What do you mean?" I asked.

"We still have the hearing tomorrow," he answered.

I was horrified. "Don, I can't keep visitations with Tyler. I can't hand Madelyne over to him after what happened. I can't do it."

"I know, Megan, but we have the hearing tomorrow." I could almost hear the wheels spinning in Don's head. "You need to file a PPO (Personal Protection Order) against Tyler for you and Madelyne. Go down to Circuit Court and file it before the end of today. We can serve it on Tyler tonight so he will have it before the hearing tomorrow."

I looked at the clock. It was 1:00 pm. The court closed at 5:00 pm. "Okay. I'll call your office as soon as I get it."

I hung up and dialed my dad at his office. I explained

what was going on. My dad came home to pick me up and we raced to the courthouse. By the time we got there, went through security, filled out the paperwork, and waited for the judge, it was 3:00 pm.

I knew getting an ex parte PPO was a long shot. An ex parte PPO is when a judge signs a PPO without a hearing. Most judges don't like to sign an ex parte PPO because a PPO can be extremely detrimental to someone's public record. Our judicial system is also a big advocate on giving everyone due process meaning everyone should have his day in court. I honestly didn't know what I was going to do if the judge didn't sign the PPO.

The judge granting or denying the PPO was our family court judge so she was familiar with our case. The judge's clerk pulled me into a conference room to talk with me. She needed to hear in my own words what had happened and why I was asking for a PPO. She could tell I was nervous because she kept telling me to breathe. After I was done talking, she went back to talk to the judge. After ten long minutes, she came back out. The judge had granted the PPO!

I started crying. I hugged the clerk and ran down the hall. When my dad saw me smiling, he leapt from his chair. Victory! I knew Tyler was probably going to file an appeal but I didn't care. For the moment, Madelyne was safe.

My dad and I went to Don's office and he was gleefully giggling. He reminded us about the appeal (Tyler had 14 days to appeal) but we were expecting it. Don's secretary's husband was going to serve Tyler that evening so Tyler and his attorney would have the paperwork before court the next morning. We still had to go to court, but the motion would be dismissed.

The next morning at the courthouse, Tyler had his entourage: Heather, his step-mom and dad, and a younger woman who I assumed was Heather's daughter (who looked so thrilled to be dragged into this mess). Don and Mr. Hatch went into a conference room to talk. A short while later, Don came out and sat down next to us. He was shaking his head.

Apparently Mr. Hatch thought he could argue his PPO appeal that morning. I was only in law school, but even I knew that was not allowed. You can't just swap one motion for another. First, Mr. Hatch had to file an appeal to allow the judge time to read it. He also had to schedule an appeal with the court clerk. He also had to provide the appeal for our side so we could prepare an answer. This was basic Law 101. This guy was a moron. And it got even better once it was our turn in front of the judge.

Once again, Tyler brought his entourage to watch him get his ass handed to him in court by the judge. Don began to address the judge, but Mr. Hatch started arguing the PPO.

"I know what this is about and I have to stop you right there," the judge said, interrupting Mr. Hatch. "You have to file the paperwork and schedule a date with my clerk."

"Well, there is a whole other side to this story that *you* haven't even heard," Mr. Hatch said.

I held my breath. Was he implying that this judge, the same judge who signed the PPO, was wrong? BIG mistake. Judges do not like to be told they are wrong.

The judge waved her arm in the air. "I'm sure I'll hear all about it. Next case." And with that, she dismissed Mr. Hatch and Tyler like two little pests.

When we left the courthouse, Don reminded us not to get too comfortable because an appeal would probably be forthcoming. The countdown was on. When 14 days went by and we didn't hear anything about an appeal, we were shocked. Don said that in his 35 years of practicing law, this had never happened. They had 14 days to file an appeal and they didn't. I wanted that to be the end of it, but I knew it couldn't be that easy.

The last day of July was Tyler's first pre-trial appearance for the domestic violence and assault charge. I had heard through the grapevine that Tyler was still denying that he had done anything wrong and that my dad had gotten him arrested. That became a running joke in our house.

My dad is very well known in our city because he

used to be president of the school board and serves on many volunteer boards and committees. But to be able to exert power over the police?

I blamed myself. Apparently, I made Tyler watch too many episodes of my favorite TV show, *The Sopranos.*

The city attorney asked if my dad and I could attend the pre-trial conference so she could talk to us about what had happened and how we felt moving forward. When we arrived at the courthouse, I was surprised to see Tyler, Heather, and Mr. Hutch. Usually, attorneys practice one specific area of law but apparently Mr. Hutch was a jack-of-all-trades. Not only was he Tyler's family law attorney, he was also Tyler's criminal defense attorney.

The city attorney's assistant, Emily sat down with my dad and me in a conference room. She was extremely helpful and wanted to make this process as easy as possible for us. She explained that Mr. Hutch was probably going to try to work out a plea with the city attorney and this case should be wrapped up by the end of August. I told her that was fine because I didn't want things to drag out. My dad and I slipped into the courtroom to watch the proceedings. We expected the city attorney to ask the judge to set a sentencing date because we figured both sides had worked out a plea. Of course, we should have realized that, with Tyler, nothing was ever that easy.

"Your Honor," began Mr. Hutch, "the first issue that we need to address is that my client has not been able to see his daughter since the day of this unfortunate incident. We ask that the court allow my client visitation provided that a third party do the exchange with Ms. Cyrulewski."

My jaw literally dropped. This was the reason why they didn't file an appeal in regards to the PPO. They were trying to circumvent the circuit court's ruling by appealing to this *district* court judge to allow visitation! This was so unbelievably unethical!

And once again, Tyler made it seem as though I was the problem, not him. It didn't matter if a third party did the exchange because, ultimately, Madelyne was afraid of Tyler but Tyler would never admit that. Not in a million years. I almost stood up to say something when I saw the city attorney jump up from his seat.

"Your honor, are you aware there is a PPO signed by a circuit court judge in this case barring the defendant from any contact with the victim and the child?"

The city attorney approached the bench and gave the judge a copy of the PPO. The judge looked over the paperwork and shook his head.

"I'm not comfortable overruling anything signed by a circuit court judge. This PPO is not my jurisdiction, therefore, I cannot allow visitation with the minor."

Whew. My dad and I clasped hands. Oh, but Tyler and Mr. Hutch weren't finished. "Next, your honor, we request a copy of Ms. Cyrulewski's medical records. She was hospitalized on several occasions in the mental health ward and we need to know her state of mind at the time she attacked my client."

Were they serious? Did they honestly think they were going to be able to get my medical records? For a misdemeanor domestic violence case where I was the victim? Who were they kidding? I knew it was a tactic to scare me into telling the attorney to drop the charges, but I didn't have to be in law school to know that to get access to someone's medical records was almost impossible.

And they were already laying down the groundwork to show that I was unstable, saying that I had been in the mental health ward "numerous" times. I was there three times, people. The third time was overnight so I don't even count that as a visit. Thank God I did not put Tyler's name on those HIPPA forms. The judge set a new hearing date to allow arguments on whether or not my medical records should be allowed into evidence. That was standard procedure, so I wasn't worried.

When my dad and I left the courtroom, Emily caught up with us. She wanted to make sure I was okay. I was fine because I was used to this shit from Tyler and his attorney. As my dad and I rounded the corner to leave the courthouse, Tyler, Heather, and Mr. Hutch stood in front of the only exit so we would have to pass them in order to leave. This was yet another juvenile tactic to intimidate.

We went to Don's office after court to fill him in on the proceedings. He agreed that it was all a big show to scare me. Don said they would never be able to get their hands on my medical records. He also said the longer they stalled the better it was for us. I completely agreed. Before we left, Don said to keep him updated but he didn't expect anything else to happen in regards to the PPO or parenting time case. Once again, though, we could never underestimate the idiocy of Tyler and Mr. Hutch.

The next day, I received an e-mail from Don. It was a motion for parenting time made by Mr. Hutch. Apparently, when his tactic to try to get visitation from the district court judge didn't work, *on the same day*, he filed a motion to appeal with the circuit court. I guess he was banking on the district court not knowing about the PPO and granting visitation. He stated in his brief:

- That as a result of a personal protection order, all parenting time with his 18 month old child has been stopped.

- It is in the best interests of the minor child that parenting time be reinstated pursuant to the last Friend of the Court recommendation.

- Given the existence of the PPO and contingent upon the court making provision

in the PPO, Defendant requests specific parenting time with a third party drop off.

Just when I thought Mr. Hutch couldn't be more of a
moron, he pulled something like this out of his ass. Did
he really think our judge, the judge who signed the PPO,
was going to say, "Good idea? A third party drop off is
the best solution. The PPO is dismissed." Really?
Don's answer to the brief was simple and straight to
the point:

Since the last Friend of the Court
recommendation has been issued, the
defendant has been charged with the
crime of domestic violence and is under
a bond from the district court, awaiting
trial. Thus, the Friend of the Court
Family Counselor does not have the information concerning that incident.

Duh.
A couple of days later, I received a huge packet in
the mail from Mr. Hutch. He sent me and Don his brief in
support of modifying the PPO. Out of respect for Don,
Mr. Hutch just needed to send it to him, not to me. But it
was yet *another* tactic to try to scare me off the case. The
brief was ridiculous:

The parties were married and subsequently divorced in 2011. They share legal custody of Madelyne, born 12/02/10.

One of the causes of the divorce was the deteriorating mental condition of Ms. Cyrulewski. She was admitted to Beaumont Hospital's mental health unit on several occasions in 2011. When the parties finally divorced, Defendant began parenting time. Although his parenting time was limited, Ms. Cyrulewski has interfered with that parenting from almost day one.

Finally, Defendant had enough interference with his parenting time and filed a motion on January 19, 2012, requesting an increased parenting time schedule. In February of 2012, the parties met at Friend of the Court and came up with a parenting time schedule that was agreed upon. Defendant began a series of supervised visitations at HARBOR and was given some unsupervised visits at the end of the HARBOR visits. This was embodied in an order. Ms. Cyrulewski inserted herself even into this scenario by insisting that she attend at least the first couple of HARBOR meetings.

On March 1, 2012, Ms. Cyrulewski

emailed Defendant and indicated that
"...because I will tell you right now, when
you are allowed to take her out, and she cries
when we meet to exchange her, she is NOT
going with you."

Shortly after this, things seemed to settle
down. There was a review on June 7, 2012, at
which the parties came up with a further
agreement to expand the parenting time. At
around the end of June, Defendant's attorney
contacted Ms. Cyrulewski's attorney in the
divorce case. Defendant was seeking the ex-
panded parenting time that was recommended
on June 7, 2012. Ms. Cyrulewski refused to
allow this Friend of the Court recommendation, which was agreed upon, to be embodied
in an order. A motion to adopt the recommendation was scheduled by Defendant's attorney for July 6, 2012 (actually, it was for
July 10, 2012).

For a couple of weeks, the parties were
able to exchange without any problems.
However, Ms. Cyrulewski decided unilaterally that she wanted Defendant to sign a different parenting time agreement, once more lim-
iting the parenting time. He refused.

At one of the Sunday drop-offs, Ms.

Cyrulewski found out that Defendant was living with his fiancé. She became enraged. She sent a text indicating that she was angry and upset that Defendant was getting married so soon.

It is no coincidence that on June 29, 2012, Ms. Cyrulewski unilaterally changed the meeting place for the exchanges to the Troy Police Station. Defendant complied. Finally on July 4, 2012 (actually, it was July 8, 2012) the parties met as scheduled at the Troy Police. Unfortunately, Madelyne was cranky and both parties worked to calm her down. Finally Defendant put the child in the child car seat. At about that time, Madelyne started to cry again.

True to her communication back on March 1, 2012, Ms. Cyrulewski became enraged and tried to take the child out of the car seat. Defendant inserted himself in between the open rear car door and Ms. Cyrulewski. She began pushing Defendant to try to get to the baby. Her father soon came over and intervened and attempted to try and push Defendant out of the way.

It is believed that the actions resulting in this PPO and the criminal complaint that un-

derlies it, were *preplanned* by Ms. Cyrulewski. She has graduated law school and has
made it very clear to Defendant that he will
not be a part of this child's life. She is carry-
ing out that plan.

Although it is troubling that this incident
took place in front of this child, this was in-
stigated by Ms. Cyrulewski's actions in trying to take the baby away from Defendant on
his court ordered visits. Obviously, this was
an emotional and ongoing situation.

Defendant seeks to modify the PPO and
the parenting time and to make provisions for
a third party to do the pick up and drop off of
the minor child.

Wow. So was the paragraph about how I preplanned
the entire event Mr. Hutch's *Perry Mason* moment? And
if I did preplan everything, then everyone had to be in on
it, including the police, the district court judge, the city
attorney, our family court judge, and her clerk.

I actually hadn't graduated from law school yet and I
was glad because I took this brief into class and my
classmates had a ball reading it. My professor asked if he
could make a copy to show his colleagues because according to him, "They would never believe me."

Attorneys are supposed to advocate for their clients,

however, not at the expense of blatantly lying to the court.

Then, if that wasn't bad enough, Don received yet *another* motion from Mr. Hatch a week later. He wanted an evidentiary hearing regarding the modification of the PPO because, "Unfortunately due to changes in personnel at this counsel's office, this matter was not filed within the 14 days but instead was filed after 18 days."

Nice. Can't find a legal reason why you didn't file in time and you can't lie to the judge and tell her you tried going around her back to the district court judge, so now you blame your staff? This was Ethics 101. Attorneys are responsible for the staff in their office. So if the secretary didn't file something on time that means *you* didn't file something on time. Also, Mr. Hatch lied about the number of days. Again, lying to the court is not a good idea.

Don's response was, "Defendant's motion is not 18 days late, but 25 days late. Either way, by statute, more than 14 days has lapsed since service was made."

Unless Mr. Hatch had newly discovered evidence as to why he didn't file an appeal in the time allowed, he was not going to be able to modify the PPO. Nevertheless, Mr. Hatch scheduled a hearing for August 10, 2012. I really didn't want to go to court again. I knew they couldn't make a case, but there was always that slim possibility that the judge would give them something. Don told me if Tyler was going to get any parenting time, it would be supervised until the criminal case was over. I figured I could live with that.

The morning of the hearing, my dad and I were getting ready to go to the courthouse when I got an e-mail from Don's secretary. Mr. Hatch cancelled the hearing! I honestly don't even remember the last time I felt that happy. The PPO would be in effect for one year and there wasn't a damn thing Tyler or his attorney could do about it. Tyler was not only prohibited from visitation, he was not allowed to contact me through e-mail, text, phone or even a third person. So even Heather couldn't contact me or Tyler would go straight to jail. One whole year without having to deal with Tyler. It truly felt like a gift from God. The timing couldn't have been more perfect.

The first three years of a child's life are the most important developmentally. Even if Tyler wanted visitation when the PPO expired, he would have to do a minimum of six months supervised visitation, which would take Madelyne past her third birthday.

From the time Madelyne was born, I had been living a nightmare. Now, there was no more wondering what Tyler was going to do. No more checking my e-mail 100 times a day. No more clenching my teeth and counting down the minutes every Sunday during visitation. Finally, for the first time in almost two years, I could breathe.

Chapter 13

I Am Free

I have had a lot of people ask me if I wished I had never married Tyler. Not for a minute. Without Tyler, I never would have had Madelyne. What I do wish is that Tyler had taken the chances offered to him throughout his life to seek the help he so desperately needs.

For almost two years, Tyler tried to convince everyone that I was trying to keep him away from his daughter. The biggest irony of the entire situation was that I was actually Tyler's biggest advocate. Even though I definitely sent my share of nasty text messages to Tyler, those messages were about my personal feelings toward him as a terrible husband. I begged Tyler to be in his daughter's life. I felt that it wasn't my choice to take Madelyne's father away from her. If I had truly wanted to keep him away from Madelyne, I never would have invited him to my parent's house to keep visiting Madelyne even after the divorce was final. I wouldn't have called Tyler to update him after each of her doctor's appointments. Even though I couldn't *stand* to be around him, I spent as much time with him as he needed at each of his visits to answer any questions about Madelyne.

The reviews I insisted on putting into the divorce decree were not because I wanted to "keep tabs" on Tyler. I just wanted Tyler to be deemed fit to take care of Madelyne by the Family Court. As all parents know, since the day our child is born, our first and most important job in this world is to protect our child. I wanted Tyler to be able to take Madelyne out of my house and bond with her not because he was entitled to under the law, but because he wanted to help raise her. Unfortunately, Tyler was so caught up in himself, he focused on his rights as a parent, not on his privilege of being a father.

I am far from an expert in the field of psychology, but living with Tyler and seeing him act in certain ways, I definitely know that he has NPD. Unless he seeks treatment, he will never be able to have any type of relationship not only with his daughter, but with anyone, except for Heather whom I also believe has NPD. Tyler was, at one point, making progress toward increased visitation with Madelyne. He was in therapy, attending NA meetings on a regular basis, and reconnecting with his friends and family. Then he met Heather. When I found out that Tyler was dating a single mother, I was actually thrilled. I felt that even if I couldn't trust Tyler with Madelyne, at least I could trust this woman he was dating. Then *I* met Heather. Tyler's friends were ecstatic about Tyler picking himself up after the divorce and finally facing those issues that caused the divorce in the first place. Then *they* met Heather. Now, Tyler and Heather only have each other yet they blame everyone else for their situation.

I think the biggest obstacle in dealing with someone with NPD is that they are not rational thinkers. They believe that if something goes wrong in their life, then the world is against them and someone, anyone else is to blame. Tyler doesn't have a relationship with his friends, dad, step-mom, me, or his daughter because we all feel that Heather is a bad influence on him and none of us want to be around either one of them.

Don't get me wrong. Tyler definitely had his issues before Heather entered into the picture. Natalie, Tyler's ex before me, summed up him in the most perfect way. "When he's good, he's good. But when he's bad, he's really bad and unfortunately the bad far outweighs the good."

I think that Tyler still had some of that good left in him until Heather entered the picture. I feel that she sucked all the good right out of his soul and he's just an empty shell of what he could have been.

There are days when I feel incredibly angry and resentful toward Tyler because he helped create this child but he has never taken any responsibility for her. I mostly feel that anger when I'm too tired to get out of bed but I don't have a choice because my child needs me. I feel resentment when my parents and I are almost crawling into bed at night sometimes because we're just so damn tired.

But there are also days when I feel incredibly sad because I *know* how much joy Madelyne would bring to Tyler's life. I see Tyler in her. She has his sense of humor. She can make anyone laugh until their stomach hurts and tears stream down their face. She loves the water and so do Tyler and I. I know how much Tyler would love to take her swimming. She loves to play guitar, just like Tyler. She strums her little guitar and sings songs. I know Tyler would have a blast playing guitar and making up songs with her.

As hard as this might be hard for Tyler to believe, I don't wish him any ill will. If he's happy, that's great. He married Heather and, in doing so, he made his choice between his daughter and his wife and now he has to live with the consequences of his choice.

About six months after I was able to get the PPO, I began to receive phone calls and e-mails from Tyler's friends, telling me to keep Madelyne away from Tyler and Heather.

Separately, Tyler and Heather each have their own anger issues and drug problems. Together, they are too destructive to be a positive influence in anyone's life. If Tyler and Heather stay together, that is Tyler's decision, but it will be Madelyne's decision to see Tyler *after* she turns 18.

Almost three years after moving in with my parents, I still live with them. We have settled comfortably into our roles not only as three adults living in the same house but also as Madelyne's providers, protectors and, most importantly, her family. It has been difficult at times because, with three adults, comes three different parenting styles. At times, I have had to take a stand against my parents for something I want for Madelyne. It's hard because I don't like confrontation, but at the end of the day, I am Madelyne's mother and I have to stand my ground. On the other hand, my mom's advice is invaluable and she is on my side when it comes to discipline because my dad is a huge softie.

Luckily, Madelyne has my dad as a male role model, and she is definitely Grandpa's girl. Madelyne loves to tell everyone that Grandpa is her best friend. (Twenty-seven hours of labor means nothing to this kid.) Madelyne has a very fulfilling life. She lives with Mommy, Grandma, and Grandpa. My aunt Linda (a retired school teacher) comes over every Saturday to give us a break. My best friend, Alison (Auntie Ali to Madelyne) joins me on trips to the cider mill, lets Madelyne play with her dog, and comes with us to the zoo because Madelyne and Auntie Ali love the Reptile House and Mommy won't set foot in there. But we all give Madelyne the one thing she would never get from her father: unconditional love.

In return, Madelyne is very open with her feelings, gives everyone hugs and kisses, and always has a smile on her face. She is a very active little girl, involved in daycare/school, dance lessons, gymnastics, swimming lessons, and is always game to try something new. She is without a doubt, a complete blessing to our family.

Two years after my diagnosis of PPD, I was finally able to wean myself off all but two of the medications. Now I only take therapeutic levels of those two medications for my anxiety disorder. Post-partum depression is a horrible feeling and I do not wish it upon anyone. I never want to feel that way again so even though I love Madelyne, she is definitely a "one and done."

I think there is still a nasty stigma attached to PPD and that is why women are still afraid to admit that they might be suffering from it. I think a woman who seeks help for PPD is extremely brave and is stronger than she might realize. It takes an extraordinary amount of courage to admit that something isn't right about the way you feel toward your baby.

For a long time, I often confused PPD with normal feelings of being a parent. For example, if I wanted to stay in bed an extra hour in the morning because I just wanted an extra hour to myself, did that make me a bad mom? Absolutely not. It made me human. I had to remind myself that I shouldn't care what other people thought of me as a person or as a parent. At the end of the day, as long as Madelyne is happy, then that's what matters.

In one of my last therapy sessions, I finally had the breakthrough I needed in order to move on. For the longest time, I couldn't understand why it seemed so difficult for Tyler to be a parent. But my therapist said that no matter how hard I tried, I could never make Tyler be the parent I wanted him to be, and I was finally able to let go.

My daughter is my strength, my happiness, my love. We make up silly songs together. We dance around the house in fancy tutus and ballet slippers. We even watch Tigers games together and she knows to clap when they hit a home run. She is my air. She is my soul. She is my heart.

So, who am I? I am a strong, confident, independent woman. I am Madelyne's mom.

Epilogue

After filing one frivolous motion after another in his domestic-violence criminal court case, Tyler and Mr. Hutch finally settled the case in April 2013. This was almost a year after the incident took place. Because Tyler would never, in a million years, admit to what he did to me in that parking lot, he and his attorney probably would have taken the case to trial.

The idea was just so ridiculous. They were willing to take up the court's time, a jury's time, the city attorney's time, and taxpayers' money in order to defend against a charge of which Tyler was so obviously guilty.

I don't know if Mr. Hutch thought that this was the next O.J. Simpson case, but he seriously needed to be clued into the fact that this was a misdemeanor case in district court. Instead of impressing the Judge with his courtroom antics, Mr. Hutch actually pissed off the judge and was ordered to "get this case off the docket."

A week before a jury trial would have started, the city attorney called me and said that Tyler was willing to plead. In our state, there is a statute that says if a person is charged with domestic violence first offense, that person can plead guilty and agree to anger management, community service, and a year of probation. If everything was completed after a year, the domestic violence offense would be expunged from a person's public record.

Tyler agreed to plead no contest (which in the eyes of the court is the same as a guilty plea) to disorderly conduct. So instead of admitting that he committed domestic violence and taking a plea deal to get his public record expunged, Tyler decided to plead to disorderly conduct which remains on a person's public record even after the probationary period ends.

The city attorney said that the decision was mine as to whether to take the case to trial. They would back me up regardless. I didn't care what Tyler wanted to plead. I just wanted him to get anger management and I knew a court order was the only way he would ever get help.

So his plea deal was the following: court costs and fines of approximately $1,200, one year of probation, and one year of court-ordered anger management.

The last time I saw Tyler and Heather was at his sentencing. I brought my dad and my best friend Alison to court with me just in case Tyler, Heather, and Mr. Hutch were looking for a fight.

Tyler looked completely different to me. He was not the same man I fell in love with years ago. I felt nothing for him. I don't hate him. I don't love him. I just don't have the capacity in me to care about him anymore.

After Tyler's sentencing was handed down, I thanked the city attorney and left the courtroom. I didn't look at Tyler and Heather. There wasn't a need. They live in their own world.

I walked out of the courthouse and clasped hands with my dad and Alison. I smiled and I haven't stopped smiling since.

ACKNOWLEDGEMENTS

Black Opal Publishing – To everyone at Black Opal Books – you believed in me enough to publish my book and there really aren't any words to express how I thankful I am.

Dr. R. – Thank you for your guidance, patience, advice and encouragement.

Don McGinnis – You are not only the best attorney that I am so lucky to have by my side in the courtroom, you've become a second father to me. Thank you for all of the advice (legal and personal) and putting up with my numerous questions!

Natalie – My Spa Resort buddy – We've been through a lot together but I couldn't imagine my life without out. Purple Pants Surprise!

Jessica – To one of my closest friends in the world – I just can't even begin to thank you for your support, friendship, humor, love and most important, showing me how to be the best mom I can be to Madelyne. Beckett is one lucky little boy!

Alison – How do I even begin to express how much I love you? You are the best friend I've ever had and will ever have. I know how lucky I am to have you in my life, but Madelyne is even luckier to have her Auntie Ali (especially at the zoo.)

Aunt Pat – Throughout the years, you have always encouraged me whether in person or a card in the mail. Thank you for that and thank you for coming over and spending time with Madelyne. She loves seeing her Auntie Pat!

"Prince" Brendan – Thank you for never judging, always accepting and just listening whenever I needed to talk. But I'm still thinking of a way to get you back for the cheese incident…

Nicole and Stephanie – I love that you two are part of our crazy, but loving family! Oh, and I'm so happy to have "blackmail" pictures and video on you rolling on an exercise ball with Madelyne.

Aunt Linda – What would we do without you? When you come over on Saturday, I hear you play with Madelyne and it makes me smile every time. Some of my favorite childhood memories are when Jeff and I used to spend a couple of nights at your house in the summer. I can't wait for Madelyne to start making those memories too. I love you so much.

Jeff – My big brother, I looked up to you when I was younger. Now Madelyne looks up to you too and I wouldn't have it any other way. My new favorite holiday memories are watching the two of you together. I love you as my big brother, but I love you more as Madelyne's Uncle.

Mom and Dad – I have no idea where to even start with either one of you. You have shown me love and support from the day I was born. Even though I gave you some hard times (especially in my teenage years – sorry about that, by the way) your love never wavered. I would not be the person I am today without either one of you. I honestly don't know how I got so lucky to have you as my parents. If I'm half as good of a parent as both of you, then Madelyne should turn out pretty darn good. There are no words to even describe the enormous amount of love I have for you both.

Madelyne – I know that you are going to read this one day and I hope that you understand the decisions that I made. Everything I have done since the day you were born is for you. I had a life before you but I wasn't really living. I will try my best every day for the rest of my life to make sure you are protected, happy, and unconditionally loved.

About the Author

Megan Cyrulewski has been writing short stories ever since she was ten-years-old. Eventually she settled into a career in the non-profit sector and then went back to school to get her law degree. While she was in school, she documented her divorce and child custody battle in her memoirs, *Who Am I?* Cyrulewski lives in Michigan with her three-year-old daughter who loves to dance, run, read, and snuggle time with Mommy. Cyrulewski also enjoys her volunteer work with various organizations in and around metro-Detroit.

www.ingramcontent.com/pod-product-compliance
Lightning Source LLC
Chambersburg PA
CBHW060154070426
42447CB00033B/1339